Cowansville High School Mi

Cowansville High School Misremembered

By: The former students of Cowansville High School and Massey Vanier

Edited by: Linda Knight Seccaspina

Chapter 1 - Can You Ever Go Back Home?　　Pg 6

Chapter 2 – 1963 - The Year Our Memory Files Began to Disappear　　Pg 12

Chapter 3 - Fads and the Assault on the Raccoon Population in the 50's　　Pg 22

Chapter 4 - Very Short Memories of the School Cafeteria
　　Pg 29

Chapter 5 - Did You Ever want to Become a Jedi?　Pg 31

Chapter 6 - Prime Time Players of Rocket Science　Pg 42

Chapter 7 - Smoking, Punishment and Leg Slapping?
　　Pg 48

Chapter 8 - TV Shows We Loved and Will the Real Bob Bromby Please Stand Up!　　Pg 56

Chapter 9 - Babylonian Mathematics and Other Subjects

　　Pg 66

Chapter 10 - Teachers, Lap Dancing and Chiens Chauds

　　Pg 71

Chapter 11 - 99 Bottles of Beer on the Wall and Other Educational Folk Songs   Pg 80

Chapter 12 - Twisting Your Dignity Away   Pg 85

Chapter 13 - Back To the Future - Who Were Those Masked Men?   Pg 91

Chapter 14 - Mum, Apple Pie and a Whole Lot of Cheese   Pg 97

Chapter 15 - The One About Disappearing Friends   Pg 106

Chapter 16 - Rattling Your Pies in the Sky   Pg 115

Chapter 17 - School Spirit and Thoughts from Early and Late Bloomers   Pg 120

Chapter 18 - Hippies, Pasties and the "Tear-Azz" Bar   Pg 128

Chapter 19 - More Dances, More Music and the French Gals   Pg 136

Chapter 20 - Fire Drills, Loud Bells and a Whole Lot of Noise   Pg 141

Chapter 21 - Our Miss Phelps   Pg 144

Chapter 22 - Final Words From the Facebook Group- "Those Darn Kids from Cowansville High School and Massey Vanier too"   Pg 150

Chapter 23 -Dedicated to Ed Moynan   Pg 162

Chapter 24 - The 2012 Class Reunion   Pg 167

Chapter 25 - CHS Homecoming Thank You Letter -by Claudia Forster-Allen   Pg 173

Appendix A - Guest Book - Homecoming CHS 2012
    Pg 179

Appendix B - Former CHS Students Who Are No Longer With Us - May They Rest in Peace   Pg 185

Acknowledgments

This book would not have been written had it not been for the former students of Heroes Memorial and Massey Vanier joining together on Facebook to create these memories. It was nothing but joy for me to compile these bits of conversation to do some good for the school.

Proceeds from this book will go to either a breakfast or anti-bullying program at Heroes Memorial and this book is dedicated to every single one of you that contributed and to my late sister Robin Anne Knight Nutbrown.

Thanks to my forever friend Diana Ani Stokely for the cover:
GRAFIX to go
106-B N. Bell St.
Hamilton, Texas 76531
254.386.0074
diana@grafixtogo.com

Join us in conversation:

Those Darn Kids From Cowansville High School Facebook page:
https://www.facebook.com/groups/195564317192344/

Chapter 1- Can You Ever Go Back Home?

The last time I stepped inside the town limits of Cowansville, Quebec was to visit my "kitchen table mum" Agnes Rychard. Agnes is not my mother, but her door was always open to my late sister Robin and we became part of what I call her kitchen table family. Some days I wonder if some of us who have not lived there in years could go back and slip back into the old routine of days gone by? Would things be the same or are we destined to look back and talk about the memories?

Hence the discussion of the memories of Cowansville, Quebec began:

Carole Beattie- I just posted a picture of the Cowansville Main Street before most of us were born, and it looked peaceful and wonderful the way you want things in life.

Linda Knight Seccaspina - I remember being inside the Cowansville Hotel on the right when Pierre Elliot Trudeau was elected.

David Hawke- I actually voted for him the first time he ran - don't know what ever came over me?---never made that mistake again!!

Bob Bromby - It was called Trudeaumania...many were infected...most were cured over time.

Claudia Allen- Each time I go home I wander up and down the streets and remember the way it was. It has changed but it's still home, where my roots are and all that is dear. Here, where I now live, is just a place, which has filled in the time and has little meaning.

David Hawke- When I return to the Townships and see the neglected homeplace with that stupid lake that I helped build but left before it was full, it's not home, merely the place I grew up filled with fond memories. Home to me is/was the Hamlet of Kendal, ON where I raised my family, ran my business, made friends and spent 3 decades of my life before selling the house to the young lad. However in the mere 12 years since I moved to Pontypool the area has changed enough that the home feel of Kendal is starting to fade. As "Metallica" says in their song "Where-ever I Hang my Hat is Home".

Manuel Greig- I'm with Claudia. We all change, things change, we all grow older, as do all living things. Things seemed different when I came back, 16 years ago, and a lot of things had changed. But the memories I have of

Cowansville haven't changed and the things we did as kids. It's still home and it will always be home!

Claudia Allen- Aw Manuel, you are a man after me own heart. I have never stopped being homesick after 25 years here. I still have my best friend living in Cowansville and she is patiently waiting for me to come home so we can hang out and do stuff together like the old days. It doesn't bother me that the town doesn't look the same; perhaps I can change that.

Manuel Greig- Something I missed about "home" besides the friends and relatives were "Cherry Blossoms" and "Caravan Chocolate Bars".

Linda Knight Seccaspina- I am drooling here and thinking about the chocolate milk and Nutty Butty's from the Dairy on South Street.

Kelly Reagan- I guess we can all conclude that "home" is where all our good memories are, even the memories we shine up a little. Sweetsburg and Cowansville were your typical Norman Rockwell towns where a kid could roam safely 'til "dinner time" which was lunch, then off again until supper. If you came into the house when the nine o'clock curfew went off, nobody worried about you. Now, that was freedom! Those are my good memories, not the town that changed so much because of politics and politicians.

Claudia Allen- Well said, Kelly ... my feelings exactly!

Kendall Damant- After my last post, about not being able to "go home," I've been thinking about it a lot and yes, home is where the heart is (as my Dad used to say). I remember that 9 o'clock siren like it was yesterday, along with a myriad of other fond memories. I wish I had appreciated those times then as I do now! Physically, I may be in Alberta, but when I think of my childhood I'm suddenly right back in Cowansville. Kelly, you hit the nail on the head!!

Carole Beattie- Cowansville will always be my true home. We moved away many years ago but when I see pictures of people and places that I knew growing up here, they bring back many good memories so I just "know" without a doubt that no matter where life takes me, this will always be 'home' to me. I know that we live in a very different world then most of us grew up in and maybe this fact helps to paint the Norman Rockwell picture of Cowansville to me. But that is everywhere today. When I speak to people that grew up in Scarborough, they say the same thing about their home town changing so much and not for the better.

David Hawke- Guess I look at things from a different perspective. One of my ancestors left "home" in a German principality in the 1700's to emigrate to the new world colony of Pennsylvania governed by King George (?) to a new "home". Along came the American Revolution so being loyal to King George he left "home" and all his possessions to make a new "home" in the Townships. In the 70's once again due to politics, I chose to leave "home" for ON where I raised my family, operated a business and made friends in my new "home," Personally, where I raised my own family, where my kids are "home" trumps the town where I was raised in. Finally, once again due to politics, the thought of spending the rest of my life in Canada became intolerable so am making a new "home" in El Salvador.

"A place where you can live life to its fullest & be happy" that's my definition of "home"!

Kendall Damant- I'm out west and have been back numerous times; the Cowansville/Sweetsburg that I remember doesn't exist anymore. Sad, but true.

Linda Knight Seccaspina- There is no place like home- but can you really make it home again?

Bob Bromby seconds that emotion!

"Home is a place you grow up wanting to leave, and grow old wanting to get back to"

John Ed Pearce

Chapter 2 – 1963 - The Year Our Memory Files Began to Disappear

The year 1963 was a year that none of us should have ever forgotten. I already had suffered a loss on September 27th when my mother Bernice Crittenden Knight died from lymphoma at the age of 34. The months that followed were not happy ones for me, but no one could have prepared us for what was to happen on November 22nd of that year.

I will always remember the somber words of our principal Mr. Bowen on the intercom Friday, November 22, 1963. He announced to the students of Cowansville High School that John Fitzgerald Kennedy, the 35th President of the United States, had been assassinated at 12:30 p.m. Central Standard Time in Dealey Plaza, Dallas, Texas.

So my question to the CHS Facebook group was:

Where were you in school when you heard JFK died?

From what should have been a tight well-remembered incident, it somehow turned into confusion and memory loss for a lot of us and the post should have been titled:

"Do you have any clue where you approximately were on November 22, 1963?"

David Hawke-I was in Mr. Douglas's class and can't remember which subject though. It was sad news even for us Canucks!

Jean Beattie- I was sitting in a Grade 10 physics class between Tim Bousada and his then-girlfriend Elena (last name escapes me for the moment). A feeling of total shock and disbelief seemed to be experienced by all of us. The teacher, Mr. Douglas, was out of the room for a brief time, so we all began to talk about it immediately.

David Hawke- Houston we have a problem- as I was in Mr. Douglas class in Grade 11- guess we need a referee here!

Jean Beattie- As I recall, he taught physics at both grade 10 and 11. Were you in his class when the news came of JFK's assassination? I may be mistaken--it might have been chemistry class.

David Hawke - He may have been doing double duty that day but I seem to remember him being in the classroom when the news came over the intercom---of course that was just shy of 50 yrs ago and I am not really sure of what I had for breakfast yesterday! See what you started Linda!

Audrey Bromby- I was in Mrs. Shufelt's class (I think?). Everyone was shocked. I was concerned for my mother as she loved JFK. We watched all the news and funeral. We watched as John Jr. and his sister Caroline followed the funeral procession and when John Junior saluted his father's casket as it passed. It was very sad and now John Jr. has passed too!

Kenny Bay Hall- You people are young uns, as I already had 10 years of work under my belt when JFK died and I was living in Streetsville where Hazel McCallum was mayor and she is still mayor, only now they call it Mississauga.

Bob Bromby- November 22 1963..For years I would have swore that I was sitting in Mrs. McCutcheon's class (grade 8), but I see in the 64 Hylite that I was in grade 10 that school year ...63/64...

Margaret Clay Jacob- I only remember as some other of you, that the teacher seemed upset and then told us about it after the exam was over. It seems to me that it was about the time of the World Series and a lot of the boys had transistor radios to listen to that, when suddenly the topic changed. I was also in grade 10, but with my memory, I might be wrong about the baseball.

Cowansville High School Misremembered

Carole Beattie- I was already out of school by then and I had just come out of the post office. I met someone I knew on the sidewalk and she told me the tragic news. I always have found it very strange that when someone hears something that is really a 'shocker' you can remember exactly where you were at the time. It is almost as if it was imbedded in your brain forever.

Jean Beattie- MCJ: you're right about the baseball--that's how our class learned about it.

Bob Bromby- Seems awful late in the year for baseball???

Editor's Note-"I have a baseball "professor" here waving at me that there was no baseball on that day in 1963 and he was only 3 years old!"

David Hawke @Carole- It has always been said that "one remembers exactly where they were" when bad news is heard however this thread is proving that to be an "urban legend" as we have Mr. Douglas in two classes at the same time, others in different grades, even the date of the world series is in doubt---anyone got the class schedules for grade 10/11 for Nov '63?

Jean Beattie- I repeated baseball, but perhaps it was a football game?!

Jean Beattie- You know, Barbara Goettel Lacroix and I were in the same grade (not always the same class/homeroom teacher) so I'm probably wrong about grade 10! Therefore also wrong about physics, as that science was available only to grades 10 & 11, I think. However, we were definitely in a subject classroom and not our homeroom class, and Tim was sitting in front of me, Elena behind. I believe it was another boy at the back who first picked up the news, and Elena, with roots in the US, almost went hysterical.

Barbara Goettel Lacroix @ Jean - You were in the same class as me. In the Hylite you are sitting between Maureen Forster and Sandra Yates and I am standing right behind you. You were right, it was Elena Monroe!

Jean Beattie- I've been out of the conversation for several hours--didn't you say you had Mrs. Fowler as a teacher? I don't remember her! I suspected you and I were in the same class but wasn't sure which years--thanks for solving that, Barbara :)

Barbara Goettel Lacroix- Jean - that's right, and you did also.

Jean Beattie - That was grade 8, right, Barbara? She was new to the school that year, along with the Richmond brothers... Some brain cells are reviving...

David Hawke - World Series Oct 2-6 1963 Dodgers over the Yankees 4 games straight--so NOT baseball on those transistors according to Wikipedia.

Jean Beattie- Considering the time of year- I just know it was a broadcast game that absorbed all the boys' attention.

David Hawke- But what game would be being played at 11:30 am on a weekday morning?

Bob Bromby - Was it 11:30am? I thought it was in the afternoon that I heard the news and I don't recall any games being broadcast on the radio. Heck! what do I know?

I'm still thinking I was in grade 8 and must be thinking about the 'Cuban missile crisis'. Those hippie years seem to have played around with the space/time continuum.

Kenny Bay Hall- Shots rang out at 12.30 central time Nov 22, 1963.

David Hawke- 12:30 CST in Dallas = 11:30 EST in Cowansville, Quebec.

Bob Bromby- David ..Think you have that backward..EST is ahead of CST. I make it 13:30hrs EST.

David Hawke- DUH you got me had to make it morning to fit my memory LOL

Kenny Bay Hall- It was a Friday.

David Hawke- Ah, that explains it!

Audrey Bromby- Strange I remember when JFK was assassinated but can't remember where I was when I heard about Elvis or Michael Jackson.

Claudia Forster Allen- I was down in the cafeteria for some weird reason. Maybe helping prepare a meal . . people came running down and turned on the TV and we all sat and watched . It was very upsetting and we were all in shock. The first first time in history the school was actually "QUIET"

John Farrell- I believe I was in Howie Johnson's Grade 7 classroom and a girl had gone to the washroom and came back to class and told him what had happened. When I first heard that it was in Texas, first picture that flashed through my mind was cowboys, horses and open fields. To later find out it happened during a motorcade through a major city kind of made more sense.

Maureen Forster Page- I was in grade eight. The idiot of the class, cant remember who it was, laughed and was severely reprimanded.

Kendall Damant- Grade 8, at the top of the stairs. I forget the teacher's name (sorry..) but I can see her face; she had short black hair & I even remember it was a pink dress!! She came in crying her eyes out, told us & I didn't understand why it was so important, so I guess I join you in the corner, Maureen!!!

Barbara Goettel Lacroix- That's right Kendall - if you read my post further back, I mention that we were in Mrs. Fowler's class. Maureen, we were in the same class - funny but I can't remember anyone laughing. We were writing an exam & were only told after everyone finished.

Kendall Damant- Of course, Barbara; Mes, Fowler!!!!!! DUHHHHH!!!!

Kendall Damant- Out of sight, out of mind, eh Jean? That was forty eight frigging years ago!! But it's all coming back like it was yesterday. I think that we remember

EVERYTHING in our lives; the memories are in the filing cabinet, it's just a matter of finding the file, lol!

Carole Beattie @Kendall- Yeah, I once tended to agree with you but if you have been following this thread I think it blows that theory.

Linda Knight Seccaspina- When you find those files Kendall let me know how you did it. That's why I write, to keep the mind greased up and continually moving.

Kendall Damant- Too funny, Linda!

Linda Knight Seccaspina- Ahh Kendall I wish it was a joke. My memory got lost somewhere between 1985 and 1991. If you see it send it home!

John Farrell -Linda, he could send it home-but it would probably just get lost!

Kendall Damant- Here's the test, Linda; IF YOU REMEMBER THE '60s, YOU WEREN'T THERE!!

Audrey Bromby-When was the 60's again?

Editor's Note: "John Kennedy was a friend of mine as The Byrds sang, and indeed to everyone else in the world- Rest In Peace John!"

Cowansville High School Misremembered

He never knew my name

Though I never met him

I knew him just the same

Oh, he was a friend of mine

Chapter 3 - Fads and the Assault on the Raccoon Population in the 50's

David Hawke and I have fond memories of the legendary Davy Crockett, as both of us owned Davy Crockett hats and on my 7th birthday I also received a Davy Crockett cake. Today if Davy Crockett was on TV PETA would probably force the "King of the Wild Frontier" to wear a "fun fur" hat. Of course he was the man "that didn't know fear" so PETA might have had a fight on its hands.

David Hawke- It's 1954, and you're sitting in front of a mostly snowy TV screen watching the first episode of the ABC show "Davy Crockett, King of the Wild Frontier" starring Fess Parker. Little did you know that by the end of that first episode you would be hooked, as "Davy Crockett the Indian Fighter". He was a genuine Indian fightin', 'bar wrastlen', 'badassed' Tennessee mountain man.

Editor's Note- David, Tennessee is still 'badassed' as you can buy both firearms and fireworks 24 hours a day- 365 days a year and they are still 'bar wrastlen' as far as I know.

Ron Cheek-I sure remember the Davy Crockett craze. What an assault on the raccoon population! This has to be an enormous business opportunity if the Davy Crockett coonskin hat ever makes a comeback. Think of the road kill that could be recycled for profit!

Editor's Note- My nomination for the kid who "didn't know no fear" like Davy Crockett would be CHS student Dickie Miner. Miner not only had a Davy Crockett hat he wore to school, but he did things most of us would never do. Secretly, this kid was "badass" and not one of us had any idea!

One spring day in Grade 4 Dickie came to school late and was accompanied by a very concerned father. Even though the day was sunny and warm Dickie had a plaid Elmer Fudd hat on his head. His concerned father put Dickie's book bag down and took off his son's hat, like a waiter removing a silver serving cover. When the hat was removed the whole class gasped as Dickie, who had natural flaming red hair, was now sporting a Mohawk like his idol wrestler Little Beaver.

Recess came and everyone crowded around Dickie touching his head, while marveling that he would have the nerve to do such a thing. Did anyone laugh at him and make small talk behind his back? For some reason no one ever did because he was the "King of the CHS Wild Frontier".

Editor's Note- With the discussion of Davy Crockett you have to admit there was a whole lot of shakin' going on with the Heroes Memorial student body keeping up with the teen fads. So I suggested we might start a Facebook thread about the trends and the comments rolled in.

Audrey Bromby-Hmmm...can't really think of any crazy fads..

Editor's Note-American Idol or Dancing With the Stars must have been on and Audrey was preoccupied!

Carole Beattie- Pennies in our loafers was the thing I remember most. On the weekends when we didn't have to wear our tunics, huge diaper pins (or were they Scottish kilt pins?) on the cuffs of our jeans with a big hole in one knee. Of course there were poodle hooped skirts with pom-poms and yes, bobby socks and saddle shoes.

Paul Cournoyer- Crew cuts!

Audrey Bromby remembers!!- I remember my older sister in pin curls, or a pony tail and wearing bobby socks.

Granny glasses, hippie beads, desert boots, and cardigan sweaters buttoned up the back.

Ironing our hair - those of us girls with long hair used to iron it to make it straight.

Editor's Note-How about those empty orange juice cans we used to set our hair on Audrey?

Bob Bromby- The girls in 1964 would put their hair up and "plaque" it for the dance. One of the ladies will have to explain the process but the hair was hard as a motorcycle helmet and could likely have served as such had the law required one to ride on your Honda/Suzuki/Yamaha bikes that were starting to hit the streets.

Editor's Note-Hair Spray and Dippity Doo (green or pink) was the national secret Bob!

David Hawke-The Hula Hoop and bell bottoms. Big hair, Elvis haircuts, shirt collars turned up, black leather jackets, motorcycle boots with chains.

Audrey Bromby- The perfect cool dude at a 1964 CHS dance. The shirt collar turned up and a white t-shirt underneath worn backwards-kinda James Dean-ish. The Beatle haircut and Beatle boots however identified you as a supporter of the British Invasion of pop music that's suddenly all over the AM radio top 40. You can't get in the gym without running shoes Mon-Fri but but you can scuff the floor with your Beatle boots dancing to Twist n Shout at the CHS dance on Friday nights.

John Farrell-Well, The Beatles arrived in North America while we were in high school so I guess longer hair for the guys was something that was different for the time.

Claudia Allen- I remember seersucker fabric being the rage and of course, mini and micro mini skirts to go with the go-go boots! You had white ones if you were lucky.

Editor's Note- Ask me Claudia how I kept fishnet stockings, garter belt and a seersucker gingham mini skirt together without flashing the whole school at one dance. I swear I cried when The Continental Store sold pantyhose for the first time at a whopping 98 cents a pair.

Bob Bromby- GO-Go boots....drool!...Nancy Sinatra walkin' all over me...ouch!

Audrey Bromby-Does anyone remember putting streamers on our bicycle handles or folded cardboard in our spikes with a clothes pin to make it sound like a motor bike?

David Hawke- Now that I think about it I had 2 bikes, the decked-out going to town 3 speed with 26" wheels from

Handy Andy & an old reliable CCM single speed with 28" wheels no fenders for general day use.

Oh yeah streamers, cardboard in spokes, bell. horn, dual mirrors, extra lights & as piece de resistance, a continental bumper with pickup hubcap & mirror.

We wouldn't be caught dead wearing a helmet either---however unlike the lycra nerds, we had respect for the rules of the road.

Editor's Note-Everyone remember Homer Sargent's bicycle shop on North Street? CCM approved!

Bob Bromby-Wonder what one of the latte sippin', granola munchin' lycra fitted cyclist of today would think of the decked out 3 speeds of yore. Don't forget the whip antenna and the jean jacket with the self installed studs you got from the shoemaker. We were so cool!

Those little pocket transistor radios made their 1st appearance around 57-58, and remember how great the sound was?..NOT!

Linda Knight Seccaspina-I remember the day my father was carrying on a conversation with the owner of the

Cowansville Bus Depot restaurant on South Street and he was showing him my transistor radio.

The man looked at it and said,

"Arthur, this thing is going to put the juke box out of business"

My father looked at him and said,

"Are you kidding me? They will never be popular!"

I went home and put the little beige radio under my pillow and while I listened to music I thought if if the transistor radio went out of business it might be "The End of the World". Can anyone say iPod?

Chapter 4 - Very Short Memories of the School Cafeteria

Was it Monday or Tuesday that the cafeteria delicacy Beef Stew was served or was it Macaroni Soup? Every week without fail; the mimeographed menu was circulated like a wanted poster from the Wild West on the walls. No matter what treat was served up for the day; we lined up along the basement wall of the new wing each day hoping it might be hot dogs.

For a whopping 50 cents; we were entitled to have about 15 minutes to eat our interesting meal that came with either white or chocolate milk from the Cowansville Dairy.

The worst part of the whole ordeal was to have the teacher of the day scrutinize what we were shoveling into the trash. Too much off the plate got you a scowl that you remembered for the rest of the week. Sometimes that scowl turned into words you just didn't need to hear to brighten up your day.

Sadly, I can't seem to remember any food fights, and that's kind of sad, because those grayish hot dogs would have made excellent projectiles. In High School I never went out for coffee like some; as I found it kept me awake for the afternoon. As William Shakespeare kind of wrote in King Henry the V:

They gave us great meals consisting of beef, iron and steel so we would eat like wolves and fight like the devil. Did we?

Chapter 5 - Did You Ever Want to Become a Jedi?

When I was 9 years-old my Mother told me that I become a great fashion designer as she watched me design clothes for my Katy Keene paper dolls. Fashion in those days was very important to me and when I was 15 I told the Vice-Principal I wanted to be a fashion designer. As he laughed and patted me on the head he told me girls only became either teachers or nurses.

From that point I became driven and succeeded in my mission to be the best I could be. I often think if I had to do it all over again I would have stayed in school and became a stewardess, but I don't know if I could have smiled that much all day long.

While not a huge Star Wars fan; I still might have considered being a Jedi later on and when I took the test I was told I was a prime candidate to take over Luke Skywalker's role with 79% wisdom, 31% aggression, 50% power, and 77% morality. Right!

So this week's trivia quiz was:

What was Your Ambition?

What you really became?

What you wished you had done?

Jean Beattie- If I remember correctly, my ambition was to become a writer. I really became a school secretary, and I would like to have become an occupational therapist.

David Hawke- According to the Hylite, I wanted to be an agricultural engineer and it also listed my pet aversion as 'school'; the aversion won!-----my extracurricular activity in high school was booking passengers to fill the extra seats on the sports trip bus. Little did I know that would lead to being an owner/operator of a small fleet of school buses ------what I wish I had done? Exactly what I did!

Barbara Goettel Lacroix- My ambition was to become a Secretary and I became a Secretary (now called Administrative Assistant) and so I did, and am doing, what I wished.

Valerie Ethier Cameron- My ambition was stenographer (remember shorthand?), but somewhere along the way, I became a mom, and started a day care in my home to stay with my kids. When they didn't need me so much, I did lots of part time work in retail. Then I got a great job at our local newspaper and wanted to go to U. of Guelph to study English. That had to be revised when I found myself divorced, and went to work at Moore Business Forms. There I did janitorial, plate making, and finally was able to do composing, drawing forms, etc. which I loved. Then, when the company eliminated my job, I drove the Shoppers home delivery truck and went back to doing janitorial. No one else wants to do it, and it pays well for part time. I also enjoy quilting, though I've given up the dream of having my own quilt store.

Kelly Reagan- Let's see..graduated in '56, which is 56 yrs. ago. My ambition was probably to be a grown up. What I really became was an old woman who never grew up. What do I wish I had done? Write a famous novel that was made into a fab movie and be the recluse author who never gave interviews.

Audrey Bromby- I had always wanted to go into nursing. Instead, I got married and started a family with the wrong person. I eventually got into office work. Took the two year customs broker's course and after working for a broker for a few years and ended up the Traffic Manager at Canadian Liquid Air...I wish I had become a rock star!

Claudia Forster Allen- I believe that I just wanted to get out of school. Then it was a windy twisty road by being a "bar maid" for several years, then a school secretary. Eventually met my husband, married (thought I was going to be single as I really didn't want to get married). Children came along and we moved to PEI. I was a stay at home mother and worked part time jobs for about 12 years. I went to culinary school and took Pastry Arts (as I had never gone to college or university and I wanted to graduate from more than High School . I retired for two years and got bored so I found a job that I will keep till I really retire making Chocolates and cookies at the Cow's/Anne of Green Gables Chocolate Factory. Dream job. What was the question again? I had always wanted to be an archeologist on a dig in Egypt as ancient history was my thang....but I am happy I did what I did and have never been bored.

Bob Bromby -As a teenager I wanted to be a jet pilot and the recruiting office informed me that the tests I had taken indicated I would be more suited to driving a tank. I studied electronics instead and went into the computer field as a tech in 1968. Forty years later I retired having installed, diagnosed and repaired everything from IBM unit record equipment to main frames and then servers and storage devices. Like my sister- I should have become a rock star. Money for nothing!

Audrey Bromby- Umm..come to think of it. I should have gone to San Francisco with flowers in my hair and become a hippie.*sigh*

Claudia Forster Allen- A great idea Audrey, but I went out west backpacking with the filthy people with long scraggy hair, unwashed bodies, dirty feet, bad breath and the filthiest toilets I've ever seen . . gawd almighty, I knew I wasn't suited for that life.

Audrey Bromby- But I would have become a hippie in a 5 star hotel!

Claudia Forster Allen- I would've done that Audrey, but I didn't like it that they rarely washed and their feet were really dirty and gosh, what about any kind of cleanliness. . . I say this as we went out to Calgary backpacking and the hostel sickened me . . filthy yuk! I couldn't take it. . . lol maybe if I had the flowers in my hair it woulda helped.

Audrey Bromby@ Claudia- I moved your above comment from below..it was in the wrong place...what are you smoking??

Audrey Bromby@ Claudia - I guess I was a wannabe hippie lol...had the bell bottom pants and the suede vest with the fringes...just didn't want do the no bathing thing lol.

Linda Knight Seccaspina- Sorry Claudia- I need the mints on the pillows and the clean towels!

Claudia Forster Allen- I'm smoking chocolate today, Audrey! Linda, thank God someone else is thinking like me . Hell, maybe we're making those mints on your pillow!

Linda Knight Seccaspina- I camped ONCE in my life and then divorced the sucker!

Claudia Forster Allen- Linda you nut!

David Hawke- I took a camping trip down to PEI once when you still had to take the ferry & Stompin' Tom's school house at Skinners Pond was still open to visitors.

Claudia Forster Allen Did ya freeze your butt off? Did the black flies get ya? Did the mosquitoes bite? Some will fly off with you they are so big . . were the outhouses open? They only open on Father's day . . ummm does that make sense? Sure do hope you had a grand ole time there David me man! lol byes o byes. . .

David Hawke- I went the last week in August, weather was good, no skeeters or black flies that I remember, had an awesome church lobster supper, stopped in at a county plowing match, even went by Anne of Green Gables house. Cool trip all in all, stopped in at Brome Fair on the way back to Ontario.

Sheila Perry- I believe in the Hylite I put down I wanted to become a Nurse-and that I did. Spent 2 years in training at the Catherine Booth Salvation Army Hospital in Montreal and then 32 years at Brome Missisquoi Perkins and a couple of yrs in Nursing Home in Knowlton-did some private duty and pallative nursing care. Got married and had 4 beautiful daughters-got divorced and after 9 yrs. married again to Walter Shufelt-moved to New Brunswick. Still doing pallative care for a Home Health Agency 3 afternoons a week!

Sheila Perry-I wish I would have traveled more and wish I'd have taken the opportunity to become a secretary in a Dr.'s office when I had the chance! Also wanted to be a hairdresser but glad I decided to be a nurse!

Bob Bromby - I always got a chuckle when in the older movies whenever a computer was shown, and the operators and techs were always walking around in white lab coats and carrying clip boards and when the computer was 'thinking' they would show a bank of tape drives spinning their tape reels back and forth. I never had a white lab coat in 40 years in the business and years ago repaired those tape drives and trust me...they were dumb! Now on programs like 'Criminal Minds' 'CSI' and 'NCIS", despite the "mouse" and touch pads they still cliky clak away at the keyboard when manipulating photo images... I bet in the background there is a 60's era tape drive thinking the problem through..Bet medical pro's find those doctor/hospital programs just as humourous.

Kelly Reagan- Yeah, Bob, and what you can carry in your hand now used to occupy a whole room, big room at that. Us oldies who grew up in houses with no electricity, wood stoves and walking to school (yup waist deep snow), phones if you were lucky that were "party lines" and I could go on and on....now can maneuver our way around the internet, carry cell phones and iPads. We are such a cooool generation, aren't we?! We've seen it all, done it all and most of all know how to survive.

Bob Bromby - Kelly and all - Good point Kelly! We went from big wooden telephone boxes with hand cranks to cellphones that will locate the closest Starbucks, listening to Mr. and Mrs. North radio program to 200 channels of nothing on worth watching, having a pen pal in some distant place to email and Facebook and Youtube, screaming across the Farnham Flats with the pedal to the metal with bald tires on the jalopy to have the modern car park itself...........We've certainly endured a lot of change....mind boggling, really! Some of the careers we may have fancied way back when are no longer around and a lot available now didn't even exist....I've been away from my field for 4 years and my skills are obsolete.

David Hawke- One thing we did learn that the kids of today don't is "mental & rapid arithmetic" so when we or someone else pushes the wrong button on a calculator/cash register the error is obvious.

Bob Bromby@ David-They may be returning a little to the old way now. Our grand daughter (4 1/2) is reading at the same level that the old grade 1 we attended and is even doing very basic multiplication that it seems we were doing in grade 2. She can do things on the iPad that baffles her grand dad (me) the old computer expert. Granted a lot may be due to the technology available today. Makes one wonder what the world will be like when she reaches her grand dads age..Our generation would have been baffled had we been magically transported from the 60's to present day.

Kendall Damant- My original goal was Air Traffic Control and my predicted probable employment (as I recall from the '67 Hylite) was "sweeping the runways at Dorval"

Predicted probable employment (as I recall from the '67 Hylite) was "sweeping the runways at Dorval"

My career was with Air Canada in the cargo division, first in Dorval then Calgary. The funny part is that after I retired from AC, I found myself to be bored and got involved with the Calgary Airport Authority escorting construction & maintenance crews air side to, simply put, keep them safely away from the airplanes. Occasionally, a little mud or some stones can be left behind which means I occasionally "sweep the runways in Calgary." I chuckle to myself EVERY time I do that!! Lol

I feel that I fulfilled my ambition to just be happy.

What did you want to be when you grew up?

The number one answer for the past thirty years was: "taller"! Then the next answers were: Artists, Pro-Athlete, Astronaut, Teacher, Lawyer, and Movie Star. No matter what you became you did what you could and as the sign says," you didn't put the key to your happiness in anyone's pocket"

You did it all by yourself!

Well some of us needed a little help from our friends as we sure said the darnedest things in those Hylites!

Chapter 6 - Prime Time Players of Rocket Science

Last week on the Cowansville High School Massey Vanier graduate John Staton asked us to name a building in Cowansville that he picture-posted on Facebook. After 79 comments everyone seemed to agree that it was the Nesbitt Residence on South Street but as John told us:

"No cigar!"

People argued and the Facebook page went rampant with comments:

Claudia Allen-That is the Nesbitt Residence or I'll eat my shirt! GK Nesbitt was the owner and builder of the house and the old flour mill that was on the river.

Kendall Damant-The Nesbitt Residence is the only house that even looks remotely like the picture!

John finally gave in and gave us all the correct answer:

"In the 1880's 3 wealthy families had a competition to see who could build the most beautiful house. There was the Nesbitt House, the featured house which was the Baker's I believe, and the Dr. Pickel house next to the BMP where the new wing is now. All were very similar size and style, but the Nesbitt House is the only one remaining. This house was across the street from the Robinson residence, beside Dale Morrison's house.

The Nesbitt House, this one, the Baker's I believe, and the Dr. Pickel house were all built in similar size and style. The Nesbitt is the only one remaining and photo above was taken from a Ville de Cowansville promotional brochure and the house was torn down between 1968-1970. Is it just me or does the text of the brochure make it sound like it is still there?"

I didn't go to school with Mr. Staton but realized right away he was smart and probably was the "Bobby Perkins" of Massey Vanier High School.

I remembered being in the gold star group in Grade 1 and then briefly came in second to Marianne Terrauds in Grade 5, who was a triple threat excelling in just about everything. After that if I passed a grade I kissed my Heroes Memorial lucky stars. So my personal quest for this week was to find out who everyone thought the brainiacs were of CHS and 154 comments later we had our winners.

Audrey Bromby-Mitchell McGuigan went on to be a university professor, as did Annabelle Dryden. Both Dickie

Miner and Philip Schneider turned out to be big shot lawyers. Philip is still in Montreal I believe.

Bob/Jeff Bromby-Dr Daniel Glenday PHD

Kendall Damant-Ronnie (Ron) Browning always got great marks. I saw him at a CHS reunion, I think it was in '92. He was working somewhere in the north-east states for a company involved in producing weapons.

Claudia Allen-Jimmy (Jim) Manson, PHD in History and a professor out there somewhere in the Townships. Bishops?

Jean Beattie-Ronald Browning was the smartest kid in my classes. He usually came first, with marks in the 90s. Then there was Dawn and Jill Cady, and one of them is a psychiatric nurse in Montreal.

Manuel Greig-Lynne and Larry McCrum were smart folks. Sandra Lee and Catherine Bradford, they were smart kids.

John Farrell-I would say Nancy Howard and Marianne Terrauds were both pretty smart. I remember back in grade 6 with Mrs. Bidwell that she said according to the I.Q. test results that Nancy was the smartest girl in her class and that I was the smartest boy.

Obviously, a flawed test. Although, at the time Nancy and Marianne were 1-2 in the class but I was lucky to crack the top dozen. So, maybe I didn't apply myself. Wonder if she (Bidwell) ever got in trouble for revealing that info?

Kenny Bay Hall -Well I was at CHS in the 40's, we had many young Japanese students from Farnham Internment Camp, who were extremely intelligent and very nice kids.

David Hawke-Likely some of the ones that left CHS for the trade school in Waterloo were actually smarter than some that went on to get a BA. Although at the time it wasn't thought so.

Bob/Jeff Bromby -Academic accomplishments aside, some of the smartest people I knew didn't go on to higher education.....and some left school before graduation. All depends on the measurement being used to determine "smart". Dawn Cady and Paul Comeau were the best students I went to school with, but if there was a 9/11 type attack on CHS I would follow Richard Bilow to safety !

Linda Knight Seccaspina-Jill Cady, Bobby Perkins and all the rest mentioned might have been the smartest kids; but I agree with Bob Bromby. If I was in some disaster of film epic proportions, Richard Bilow would be the first one I would follow.

If anyone remembers Richard Bilow he was the class clown, or was he really just trying to fit in? In Grade 8 he measured exactly 'not very tall' and he was always smiling. No matter what they did to this poor kid, he laughed it off and carried on like a trooper.

One day some of the kids grabbed him and hung him by the shirt collar on one of the coat hooks in the hall. His feet did not touch the ground and he almost choked to death. When he was finally unhooked they attempted to hang him on a ceiling air filter that looked like a bird swing in the centre of the room.

Not a word was said by Richard Bilow and as usual he shrugged it off, but deep inside I knew that he was secretly planning for a huge coup years later. I still believe today that Mr. Bilow was really some sort of superhero like Clark Kent, but he just never managed to get his suit off to reveal his hidden super powers.

As Ralph Waldo Emerson said,

"Common sense is genius dressed in its working clothes"

Cowansville High School Misremembered

Ain't that the truth?

Chapter 7- Smoking, Punishment and Leg Slapping?

This week I wanted to know what the worst thing CHS students did in school as none of us were angels. When I began writing this I asked a few local neighbourhood kids what they had done in school. Times have most certainly changed and when one told me he had lived in detention until Grade 10; I had no trouble believing him in schools where guns are now confiscated.

One teenager told me he jumped out of a school window in Grade 6 and got a huge gash on his leg because of his crazy stunt. I asked him why he would do such a thing and he said because his nickname was Ninja and he did not want anyone to question his ninja skills. Another chap happily gave me the information that he had given his whole class head lice while his friend took the tires off of the principal's car and hid them around school.

Were we that bad?

Claudia Allen- I do remember an incident in Grade 9B. It was lunchtime and supervision was scarce. Two boys, who will remain nameless, were hanging out of the second floor window while dangling another smaller nameless person out the window.

Dale G. Brock- The person who was hanging out the window by his legs was Kenny Bowles, [R.I.P.] and I don't remember the two persons performing the act. The teacher on the lower floor however gave Kenny hell for hanging out the window.

Claudia Allen- I thought it was Corwyn Chan. RIP Kenny. Wouldn't you know he would get heck for hanging out the window!

Claudia Allen- As to the two dudes hanging him out there to dry- Was one of them Manuel?

Claudia Allen - Perhaps you will remember this Dale. Gord, Brian Brown, yourself, and a couple others, maybe Kenny - were all lined up outside the principal's office awaiting the "strap". What happened that day? Any thoughts? :)

Dale G. Brock- Well I think you might have the right day!

Jeffrey Bromby- If you never got the strap then you never did anything that bad. The strap though was like capital punishment!

David Hawke - I remember "walking" the length of the barn hand over hand on the litter carrier track to build up callouses on my hands so the strap didn't hurt too much. Hmmm, wonder why following the rules never occurred to me?

Audrey Bromby- Did any girls ever get the strap?

David Hawke- I don't know about CHS but I am pretty sure the girls as well as the boys were caned at Feller. That makes the strap seem like child's play--come to think about it I never remember anyone getting the strap past grade 7.

Editor's Note- In the 1971 Moyers Supplies catalogue they advertised straps for sale to schools for $1.50.

From Wikipedia-

The strap was used on minors in reformatories and in schools. The latter was particularly prevalent in Canada, applied to the student's hand, until abolished in 2004, but in recent times it was generally made of canvas/rubber rather than leather.

Audrey Bromby- I was painfully shy in grade school, and I think I've told this one before, but Noreen Dryden and I were messing around in Grade 2 pulling each others dresses up. I got caught and Miss Crick made me stand in the corner. I was devastated!

The only other thing I recall was smoking out of the window in Commercial class. There was myself, Joan Mewett and Murray Dover. We never got caught!

As you may remember, the Commercial class was in the dungeon beside the girl's washroom and we were left alone a lot by Mrs. Tuer. Other than that, I was a little angel in school. Yup- that's my story and I'm sticking to it!

Roberta R Barnes- I guess you better stick to that story, because I can say the same about myself - it's like we were two peas in a pod.

Claudia Allen- I was in Mrs. Tuer's class as well. Were we together Audrey?

I remember when she came to class one morning and stunk up the whole "dungeon" with skunk! She finally told us that her dog got sprayed the night before and he slept on her clothes and stunk up the whole house. Nice lady, I really liked her.

Audrey Bromby- Yes Claudia, we were in the same class. How could you forget?? Mrs. Tuer was a very nice lady, she was just absent from the classroom a lot. She used to give me a grocery list and money and ask me to go the IGA and buy her stuff. I remember the skunk incident too.

Linda Knight Seccaspina- I was no angel but would have sold my soul to be exempt from the box horses in gym.

Carole Beattie- Linda- I was petrified of the box horses too! One day I missed the box and landed on my wrist. It really hurt but he made me get up and try again. This time I didn't even try to jump over it my wrist was hurting so much. After gym class he took me to the teacher's lounge and put a 'bandage' on it. My mother took me to the doctor and an X-ray revealed that it was actually broken. I had to wear a cast for about 6 weeks !!!!

Audrey Bromby- Speaking of those box horses; poor little Alice Falcon broke her leg on one of those. She didn't want to do it but you had to do it!

Linda Knight Seccaspina- There were some things to be afraid of when we went to school sad to say.

Kendall Damant- Mr. Tyler actually frightened me as a kid!

David Hawke- Mr. Tyler was a very good principal and like Mr. Douglas a fine man. Cowansville High School lost a lot when they both left.

Kendall Damant- We were SOOO stupid sometimes!

Kendall Damant- At least I was!

David Hawke- Naw, we were just kids!

Claudia Allen- I agree with David, we were just kids! What makes me mad is that the strap was used for mischief. No wonder they finally burned it! Carole, I am so sorry to hear that about your wrist. Guess we were just supposed to suck up and tough everything out, including a broken wrist. I have broken both my wrists and it ain't funny and forget trying to jump a box horse!

David Hawke- I don't think the strap was bad as it kept the borderline kids on the good side and the mischief makers from going too far. It never hurt anyone----just take a look at the school yards today with the dysfunctional kids!

Claudia Allen- It wasn't the worst thing, but I did spend a lot of time in detention! I think it was for TALKING . . Imagine! Me! Talking!

Claudia Allen- There always seemed to be a lot of guys in there too!

Manuel Greig @ Claudia- I know one who spent a lot of time in detention! I thought I remembered you from my trips there!

Maureen Forster Page- I used to get kicked out of class for playing around and not paying attention. I used to go to the girls washroom and do my homework, not so bad of a deal. I remember standing in front of the principal in his office, petrified, and explaining myself about something that I don't remember. I absolutely can't recall what I might have done.

Maureen Forster Page: How many hours did Bob Page spend sitting in the hall on a garbage can?

Bob Bromby @Claudia- I gotta ask- what was that leg slappin' all about in gym? What did you girls do in gym class anyways? It was enough to drive a girl to hookin' if you ask me!

Claudia Allen- I really have no idea what the "slapping" legs was for, maybe circulation. When you had stick legs like mine- well, that would just plain HURT LIKE HECK! The gym teacher did say later that it was a dumb thing to get us to do!

Bob Bromby- I'm confused and it still sounds like something out of a Sacha Baron Cohen movie.

Valerie Cameron- I'm also curious about slapping legs in gym. I was in Mr. Busteed's gym class and don't remember doing anything like that.

Kendall Damant- Claudia, I'm curious too! What's with slapping legs? Improving circulation? What was the point? I can just imagine him telling the guys to slap legs in today's politically correct terms.

Editor's Note- Actually Kendall, I did some research on the "leg slapping" and today people actually get paid quite handsomely to do it. I read quite a bit about it on pages called "Discipline and Pleasure". If you take Mr. Bromby's comment of: "It was enough to drive a girl to hookin'" - it all makes sense. Leg slapping was just simple educational preparations for whatever field you might choose to work in. Case in point below!

Showgirls- The film premiered in 1995 and the quote at 00:39:46 - "Everyone back up, find some space! Start with your right leg, slap it!"

I rest my case!

Chapter 8 - TV Shows We Loved and Will the Real Bob Bromby Please Stand Up!

Claudia Allen began a Facebook thread remembering how she used to watch Hockey Night in Canada on her Grandfather's TV as no one else owned one in the immediate family. I soon remembered coming home from school and watching American Bandstand every afternoon or listening to my Mother ramble on about what soap-opera horrors were on the Guiding Light that day. These small thoughts of course got the whole group remembering what their favourite shows used to be during the CHS years.

Paul Cournoyer- I remember getting home to watch American Bandstand on ABC Channel 8- Poland Spring, Maine with a snowy TV screen.

David Hawke- I Used to watch American Bandstand, wished I could dance as well as they could and I also liked the Mickey Mouse Club with Annette.

Keith McClatchie- I hardly ever missed an episode of "Queen for a Day" and I remember being in total disbelief of some of these sob stories! Annette Funnicello and Cubby O'Brian on the Mickey Mouse Club. Do you folks remember The Adventures of Spin and Marty on The

Mickey Mouse Club and at supper time they had a different adventure/action show every day - Robin Hood, Lone Ranger, Hopalong Cassidy, etc.

Bob Bromby - Only time I got to see Queen for a Day was if I could convince my mom I was too sick to go to school or a school holiday and there wasn't something more interesting to do outside. In those days the outside usually won!

(And now a word from our sponsor - Bob Bromby's CHS Bus Complaints!)

We got home too late from school after the bus ride as the bus dropped us off at about 4:30 and then another 15 minute walk from there. We left to catch the bus at 7:30am and returned after 4:30pm. Our bus was the 1st to arrive at CHS in the morning and the last to leave at 4:00pm. The bus did a double run to Dunham so we got dropped at school in the morning and it would head to Dunham to pick them up. After school it would drop the Dunham crowd off 1st and then come back to pick us up. Could never understand why if we got dropped off 1st in the morning and then why didn't we get picked up 1st after school. You Dunhamites were a bunch of pampered woosies!

Audrey Bromby - You just forget Rocky and Bullwinkle.

Linda Knight Seccaspina-Audrey, were Rocky and Bullwinkle part of the Dunhamites?

David Hawke - Fess Parker as Davy Crockett was a must watch but as Bob says outside stuff took precedent over TV. I had the hat, vest & pants---did you know that Davy & about a dozen others survived the battle of the Alamo but as they fought under a flag of no surrender, were put to death after the battle was over!

Note from Editor-If you read the CHS chapter "Fads and the Assault on the Raccoon Population in the 50's" it describes all our hidden fur-related childhood fetishes.

Bob Bromby - The Flash Gordon serials were before TV and played in the theatres..They were broadcast on American channel 8 after school for a while. Think they were produced in the 1930's and Ms. Arden was Flash's lady. I always had a thing for Jane Arden (no not Canadian singer Jann Arden) of the Flash Gordon serials and talk about special F/X.

One of my favourites had three characters Sandy, Dusty and a third who was their comic relief. I can't recall his name. Then there was Lash Larue, Whip Wilson, Cisco Kid with Pancho-all in dazzling fuzzy B&W.

David Hawke- Then a tad later came Gunsmoke with Marshall Matt Dillon & Chester was a woman to but forget her name---mustn't forget the adventures of Palidin in Have Gun Will Travel!

Linda Knight Secccaspina- It was Miss Kitty David - Technically she died of liver failure brought on by viral hepatitis, which was AIDS-related." Blake's secret was known only to a few intimates. "Once she knew she had it, she decided to keep it to herself," says her closest friend, Pat Derby.

Bob Bromby - Gunsmoke- The barmaid was called Kitty.

Linda Knight Seccaspina-I just said that Bob! Boy we both must be mind readers today!

Manuel Greig @ Bob-Funny, when I read Jane Arden, I thought of Jann Arden and her song "Insensitive". I don't recall a Jane Arden as it must have been before my time!

Claudia Allen: We're much younger than Bob, Manuel . . haha

Editor's Note- Hmmm- How old is Bob anyways??

David Hawke- How about the first soap La Famile Plouffe?

Manuel Greig- I think all these things are before my time- or maybe before we got a TV.

Claudia Allen- I was too young too Manuel but I did hear of the Family Plouffe and think they were on the radio first.

Audrey Bromby- I loved the Loretta Young Show in the afternoons. But, as Bob mentioned, we sometimes had to (fake) be sick to stay home to watch them during the weekdays. My Grandmother used to love to watch The Edge of Night and As The World Turns. I used to sit and watch them with her when she was visiting.

Manuel Greig- I don't remember these shows. I guess I had other things to do- like being a farmer!

Linda Knight Seccaspina- I named my son after the villain of The Edge of Night - Schuyleur Whitney.

(Insert sounds of silence and birds chirping as very few name their kids after soap-opera villains except Linda!)

Editor's note-"Now Here's the Weather"- (older people's minds rattle and ramble)

Claudia Allen -Anyone remember Bird Berdan the weatherman? Bird Berdannnnnnnnnnnnnnnn?

Keith McClatchie: Bird Berdan the Weatherman from Channel 5 WIRI b4 they changed to WPTZ

Bob Bromby- Then of course there was Percy Salzman the Canadian weatherman with the chalk board. He would toss the chalk in the air at the end of his forecast.

Claudia Allen: Righto, Percy, he was a great weatherman! I remember the chalk thing!

We suddenly revisit The Mickey Mouse Club

Manuel Greig @ David -there was another on Mickey Mouse, besides Annette, can't remember her name,cute little thing...

Bob Bromby: Darlene was the blonde one and Annette the dark hair. Annette went on to those horrible Beach Party movies with Frankie. She was a role models none the less- overly naive but compared to the role models todays kids have!

Editor's Note-Bob- are we talking Britney Spears here? No!!!! Not a role model? What a shocker!

Manuel Greig @ Bob-Darlene...that be her...good man Bob!

Bob Bromby - I think Darlene went on to be a Dallas Cowgirl Manuel.

Manuel Greig @ Bob -.No, last I heard she was down on her luck......:(

Linda Knight Seccaspina - Manuel Has she hit The Enquirer yet?

Manuel Greig - Oooh ya !! Probably so, a long time ago....

Editor's Note - In December 1998, Darlene Gillespie was convicted in federal court of aiding her third husband, Jerry Fraschilla, to purchase securities. She was sentenced to two years in Federal prison. Gillespie was never seen cheerleading behind bars.

Carole Beattie- I remember we would all sit around the T.V. to watch The Honeymoons with Jackie Gleason every Sunday night and I Love Lucy with Lucille Ball. I think they were much funnier than the comedy programs they have today. The quiz show I remember was What's My

Line? and a news show with Harvey Kirk and Joyce Davidson (Can't remember the name of it now).

Editor's Note-Google does not compute Canadian television and Joyce Davidson was born Joyce Brock, used her first husband's name even after marrying (and divorcing) the late David Susskind. Ever wonder why CBC's news anchor Yvan Huneault mysteriously disappeared after a CBC newscast joke about a Basset Hound named Isabel?

Paul Cournoyer- Jackie Gleason- One of these days Alice - Pow to the moon?" Rowan and Martin's Laugh In - "sock it to me!"

Bob Bromby - Anyone old enough to remember the Dobie Gillis Show with Tuesday Weld? The beatnik Maynard G Krebs who went on to be Gilligan.

Manuel Greig- Before my time, Bob....lol

Bob Bromby @Manuel- What? Were you born in like 1980?

Bob Bromby- No one has mentioned the Howdy Doody Show. I know Manuel is too young to remember that far back.

Carole Beattie- It's Howdy Doody Time.... it's Howdy Doody time, it's Howdy Doody Time.... it's Howdy Doody Time :)

Carole Beattie- Kookie..... lend me your comb !!!! And then there was Dragnet.

Bob Bromby- Just the facts Mam!

David Hawke- Oh yeah Dragnet, looks like a young crowd here that don't remember these old shows, more into the 60's----Route 66, swore to drive it one day, finally did some 45 or so years later, highly recommend doing so!

Bob Bromby- When we 1st got a TV, the only station was CBC out of Montreal and they broadcast in French and English. The Indian head was on the screen until about 5:00pm and returned at 10:00 or 11:00pm. A kid's show with a guy with a guitar who sang to a frog down in a well would start off the daily programming.

Note from Editor-A frog in a well? What year was that Bob?

Oh heck, this concludes our broadcasting day!

Cowansville High School Misremembered

Chapter 9- Babylonian Mathematics and Other Subjects

This week's trivia question was:

"If you could have added a subject on the CHS curriculum what would it be and who would have taught it?"

Audrey Bromby- hmm..one choice would be drama...and Mrs. Blinn would have taught it.

Claudia Forster Allen- Cooking with Chef Michael Smith . . . now that's cooking!

Audrey Bromby- ummm...or Jamie Oliver...lol

Claudia Forster Allen- either or . . :)

Audrey Bromby Or even Julia Child..rest her soul.

Claudia Forster Allen- Ya, I was thinking of her as I wrote Chef Michael. That would've been a riot, let's have a drink for the chef! haha

Audrey Bromby -LOL. I'll drink to that...hic

Audrey Bromby- How about Home Reno with Bryan Baeumbler?

Editor's Note- Wait guys!!!! You were supposed to pick one of the CHS teachers and as I know Smith and Baeumble were probably not even born yet.

David Hawke- It never would have flown with the aristocratic attitude of the day but instead of the half-assed wood working "Industrial Arts"/manual training, an auto shop class would have been beneficial. there were lots of good mechanics around town that could have taught it.

John Farrell- How about Sex Ed. with Miss Spicer?...seeing how she was already there.

Manuel Greig- Phy. Ed with Jillian Micheals

Bob Bromby- Whatever it was that I was going to suggest went right out the window when I read John's suggestion of sex-ed with Miss Spicer.

Claudia Forster Allen- Here we go again . . . .lol

Claudia Forster Allen- Phys ed with Tony, built like wow . . . . the muscles on the guy, yikes!

Editor's Note: Tony Little??

Maureen Forster Page- Too funny............dreamers.

Bob Bromby- CHS Sexy-Ed....Us guys would have been with John F and Miss Spicer but unfortunately for us they would probably have assigned sexy ed to Mrs. Shufelt of grade 7 fame!

Jean Beattie- Biology, and probably no one at CHS at the time I was there. I took it later, at university, and it was fascinating.

Audrey Bromby- How about a decent health class with Dr. Oz?!

Claudia Forster Allen- I like the cute one on the panel of four doctors....can't remember the name of the show but he's a looker....

Yeah, I used to watch that one too--he is (thirties, blond, quite athletic)...

Claudia Forster- Allen Yup, that's the one!!!!!!!!

Margaret Clay Jacob- Claudia, the show is simply called "The Doctors" and the gorgeous doctor is engaged now (lucky girl).

John Farrell- Girls, quit fantasizing and stick to the question...adding a different subject to CHS. list....CHS.

hasn't been CHS. since 1969, shouldn't the teacher at least have been BORN by then? Bunch of cougars!!!

Claudia Forster Allen- Yup, that's us! hahaha, young at heart and looking is good! No touching, just looking . .. we are just improving on what was there . . how come you aren't commenting on Bob's comments about Miss Spicer being a hottie . . ummmmm?

Bob Bromby- John F is right...You girls are livin' in the present....Get livin' in the past with us guys and Miss Spicer....drool!

John Farrell- Well Claudia, Miss Spicer was actually a teacher and was at CHS so could have taught the additional subject...the fact she was a hottie, well that's just a bonus. People you are suggesting if born were still in diapers at the time. The person wouldn't actually have to be a teacher....waitress at the bluebird....maybe ticket taker at the Princess...hottie who lived next door....but they should have at least been born when the chosen subject was to be taught.

Audrey Bromby-I'd like to see Julia Child in diapers ROFL!

Editor's note- Of course I had my own opinions and here are my suggestions for unique classes to be taught by former teachers:

Mrs. Fulford: Star Trek Philosophy

Mrs. Shufelt: Zombies in Popular Media

Mrs. Luce: Learning From YouTube

Miss Parsons: Arguing with Judge Judy: Popular 'Logic' on TV Judge Shows

Mrs. McCutcheon-Daytime Soap Operas: Family and Social Roles

Mr. Douglas-The Science of Superheroes

Miss Righton- The Simpsons and Philosophy

Miss Spicer- Cyberporn and Society

I cannot take the credit for these classes as these are actual classes taught in some colleges in the United States so my question is:

What would the "Johnson brothers" have taught? Lego Robotics or How To Stage a Revolution?

Thoughts?

Chapter 10-Teachers, Lap Dancing and Chiens Chauds

We had a lot of great teachers at CHS and my question this week was: Which teacher should have gone on to bigger and better things?

Manuel Greig- Mr.Bradford...should have been a sheep-herder !!

Richard Bilow- I thought Stephen Trew had a creative approach to his teaching which would have been a valuable tool in any field.

David Hawke- Mrs. Rubens likely could have done well in the art world---can't think of anyone else---Mr. Douglas did move up to administration in Chateguay

Bob Bromby- Mrs. Blinn...I had her as grade 7 teacher. She was more than just a "get the subject matter across" , in my opinion. There were others of course but Mrs. Blinn certainly undershot her potential. Miss Phelps and Miss Welch and Mrs. McCutcheon certainly chose the right profession ...IMHO!

Keith McClatchie- First of all there were a number of teachers that I had who did great things - Miss Phelps, Mrs. McCutcheon played huge roles in preserving the history and archives of Brome County. My aunt Bernice (the infamous Grade 9 home room teacher) put her name on several Geography text books that were used in Canada back in those days. Her sister Mildred (the equally infamous Grade 6 home room teacher) Parsons (my "aunt-in-law") willed a portion of her estate to a scholarship bursary thing given out annually in Cowansville. Merton Tyler, our beloved Principal and hockey coach was involved in education in the Townships for many years. Gordon Bown went on to be pricipal and then fired by the board but he remained in education until he retired. He had a profound effect on me and traught me to love math and science. I can still remember some of his lectures. Mrs. Lewis, my Kindergarten and Grade 2 teacher was an excellent early childhood education specialist and gave me my love of reading (and writing). Even Doris Welch (Grade 10) encouraged students in her own way (quiet and unassuming) including me to pursue higher education and set realistic goals.

Kenny Bay Hall- Mrs. Bibby, my grade 3 teacher at CHS. She was gentle, kind and loving.

Audrey Bromby- The only teacher who left an impression on me was Mrs. Blinn. I had her in grade 7 and french. I have never forgotten her.

Linda Seccaspina- Mrs. Blinn should have worked for the UN.. Mrs. Bibby.. my grandmothers best friend.. loved her.. Miss Phelps.. Why was Gordie Bowen fired??

Keith McClatchie- He was let go because the board felt he was not a competent manager. He had been assistant principal for years but was only principal for a couple of years. A lot of us parents attended the meeting and fought like hell on his behalf to no avail.

David Hawke- My mother quit teaching at CHS (moved on to Stanbridge East Elementary) rather than spend a second year under Bowen as principal - nough said!

Claudia Forster Allen- Mrs. Blinn should've gone further .. an actress or a writer .. she could do both as she regaled us with all her wonderful adventures in the canoe with her father following the waterways from the North. Loved Miss Phelps and she did achieve her potential and then some. Mrs. Rubens should've been in the art world somewhere. She was a gentle soul.

Bob Bromby- Then there was the Gym teacher ..Major Reubens..who I always wonder if (1) was he really a Major and (2) if yes,in what army?

David Hawke- Canadian Army EH!

Claudia Forster Allen- always wondered the same thing, Bob. . . we'll go in search of the truth . . .:)

Paul Cournoyer- Mrs. Rubens was teaching French when I went to C.H.S. she would always ask me when she spoke French if the words she used were the right ones. Don't know where she got her diploma to teach French. Must have been the same place as her husband by mail (correspondence). Her husband was a *MAJOR* disaster when it came to sports.

Richard Bilow- So Bob there's your answer according to Paul it's not a rank but an adjective.

Margaret Clay Jacob- I agree with many of you about Mrs. Blinn. What a wonderful person and teacher. Also Miss Phelps, who was super in teaching Art class.

Pennie Redmile- Was Mrs. Reubens really a good French teacher? I only remember her telling us about her trip to see the Taj Magal. To this day whenever I hear of the Taj Mahal-- I think of Mrs. Reubens!

Claudia Forster Allen- it was rudimentary French ie le plancher sort of thing . . . not sure we heard a whole sentence but I was only in grade 4. We may have learned a little poem but it escapes me at the present. Let's face it, we didn't really have to learn French at that time. I had a nosebleed in class one day and she gave me a lovely white handkerchief to use. I didn't want to get blood on it but she told me to keep it, which I did but lost it in times gone by. . . . :(

David Hawke- I never had Mrs. Reubens for French but it must have been better French than that used on the street back in the day, remember a driver coming into the shop with his truck because "le clutch she es broke!"

Bob Bromby- Or "un hotdog all dress avec frites"...I always ordered in French at Chez Roger.

Kenny Bay Hall-Over da river across da pont.

David Hawke- Actually had un hot dog con salsa y chile piquante at a street cart outside Immigration on Wednesday. :)

Kelly Reagan- My opinionated self feels the urge to jump in here...I could never understand why the French culture who was so adamant about preserving their LANGUAGE (i.e. signage over businesses) would trash that same language with more English words in their everyday conversations than French. And from what I remember, if you did speak a good French, then that was regarded as a kind of snobbery. Couldn't live where I was born because I'd be fighting with somebody every day about something.

Kelly Reagan- Because I'm way older than anybody on here, I remember a few good ones, Miss Wells, Miss Phelps, Miss Welch, Mrs. McCutcheon - loved them, can't imagine they could have gone on to anything else - I think they loved what they were doing and us kids. Some teachers were so angry and mean, scared me. Maybe they were the ones who wished they were somewhere else and should have moved on. But that was a different time.

David Hawke @Penny- I believe it was Mrs. Reubens tales of the Taj Mahal that put it, subconsciously on my bucket list, took 50+ years but this farm-boy from the Townships finally laid eyes on that amazing site----@ Kelly know what you mean, it's a crying shame that one can never return to their home town/province/country to live. :(

Bob Bromby @ David Hawke..Is it still a Chien Chaude as we know them here...sounds tasty...the hot dog con salsa....

David Hawke- Yupper the same Chien Chaude that we know & love with Hot Dog in English on the cart, just the toppings are different.

Bob Bromby- Speaking of French-Miss Stephenson was unique if nothing else. During class she would sometimes park herself on one of the boy's laps. I was one and she embarrassed the hell out of me. She could have become a one of a kind lap dancer if she had come along 50 years later.

Claudia Forster Allen- I remember hearing those stories about her. . . :)

David Hawke- She knew her French though, she just did it "her way".

Bob Bromby- Yes, She did know her French and I was of course referring to the traditional 'lap dancing' of the people of Lapland in full historical costume.

Claudia Forster Allen- hahahahahaahaha

Carole Beattie- Thanks for bringing back memories..... I had forgotten about Miss Stephenson and the 'lap dance'.

We all experienced many boys faces turning red :) ...... Yes, she definitely could have gone to 'bigger things'..... she missed her true calling. Born too soon.

Bob Bromby- "Bigger things"....now that is funny. :-)

Carole Beattie- Haaaaa. Just staying on topic Bob....... Linda's question was 'bigger things'.

Bob Bromby- My one track mind has been engaged.. BIGGER THINGS....at the opposite end of the scale was Mrs. Shufelt (grade 7) and lets never forget 'perky' Miss Spicer...Must be old age, I'm drooling again.

Claudia Forster Allen- too much testosterone in your blood, Bob, you need to get that checked . . . haha

Claudia Forster Allen- I liked Miss Primmerman, she was a good English and History teacher. . . she did not meet her calling.. maybe she should have been a diction teacher for the hearing impaired. . . .

Audrey Bromby- I also liked Miss Primmerman. She was a great English teacher. I never much liked to read until I had her as a teacher. The book reports were killers when we had to read two books at once but I did well in her classes.

Bob Bromby- Miss Parsons should have gone on to the Olympics as a 'fast walker'. Man! She could burn up the hallways...never a leisurely pace.

Audrey Bromby- She got all that energy by trying to catch up to Mr. Henry lol

Carole Beattie- Mert Tyler (then principal) also taught us history in grade 11. He really made some of those battles come alive!!! Great teacher.

Linda Knight Seccaspina- I always think that Miss Kidd had a lot of business sense in her and could have managed a few Tim Horton's with one hand.

No matter what they did or where they went one thing is for sure they were always true to our school and that's what mattered.

Chapter 11 - 99 Bottles of Beer on the Wall and Other Educational Folk Songs

I used to ride the school bus to the basketball games in Knowlton, not because of team spirit, but because it was an "instant party in a box" to put it mildly. Others felt the same way and comments flowed quickly on the Cowansville High School Facebook page about what they remembered about the "party rock times" as the wheels went round.

David Hawke ----99 bottles of beer on the wall, if one of the bottles------"

Audrey Bromby- should happen to fall, there'll be 98 bottles of beer on the wall..

Audrey Bromby- And then there was the famous "Bang Bang Lulu"

Audrey Bromby- Then the smoochers would head to the back of the bus to make out.

Audrey Bromby- And then there was the famous "Bang Bang Lulu"

Audrey Bromby- Then the smoochers would head to the back of the bus to make out.

Claudia Forster Allen- Really? as you can see I just got home from work and don't go scrolling down the list here.

David Hawke- Bus drivers don't mind good ole bus songs or they don't last----kids today sing the same songs we did-----got to admit "the wheels on the bus go round and round" is getting long in the tooth though.

Claudia Forster Allen- I remember one ... Bang, bang Lulu, bang her hard and strong.. I never knew what bang meant and wondered why everyone laughed. .

David Hawke- Audrey already posted that, thought I said NO plagiarism there girl :)

Claudia Forster Allen- Hell, I quit . . I'm not scrolling all the way to the top . . . this is what happens when one goes out to work for 8 hours and comes home and everything is already said and done . .

David Hawke- Work is bad for you, makes one tired!

Claudia Forster Allen- and cranky in this heat...lol

David Hawke- Glad I'm too far away for the flying frying pan to get me!

Keith McClatchie- Then there was the song about Gramma's old red PJ's

Keith McClatchie- ". . . they were ragged, they were torn, around the - - - hole they were worn, they were baggy at the knees, and the - - - was full of cheese"

Bob Bromby- "'guzzle guzzle guzzle as it trickles down your muzzle..call out your order loud and clear _____ _____ "

Roberta R Barnes- hahahaha

Claudia Forster Allen- OMG, Keith, never heard that one!

David Hawke @Bob- I believe the end was MORE BEER!!! I remember singing the one Keith mentioned, guess it got stopped at the QC/ON border as never heard it again on the bus trips I did :(

Barbara Goettel Lacroix- Never heard that one of Keith's either Claudia; must have been before our time!!! Those bus trips sure bring back memories!

David Hawke- @ you youngunshttp://www.fresnostate.edu/folklore/drinkingsongs/html/catorigized-...

http://www.fresnostate.edu/folklore/drinkingsongs/html/cat origized-by-song/red-flannel-drawers-that-

www.fresnostate.edu

David Hawke- @ you youngunshttp://www.fresnostate.edu/folklore/drinkingsongs/html/catorigized-...

http://www.fresnostate.edu/folklore/drinkingsongs/html/cat origized-by-song/red-flannel-drawers-that-

www.fresnostate.edu

Kenny Bay Hall - One potato,two potato,three potato,four...NO! Wait a minute,that's not a song,that's about choosing who's it..

David Hawke- The link doesn't work but if you type it in will take you to lyrics-----Roll me over in the clover was another popular one

Kenny Bay Hall- She'll be coming around the mountain, when she comes...

Audrey Bromby- The ants are marching one by one..hurrah hurrah!

Editor's Note:

According to Wikipedia the song "Bang Bang Lulu" is a traditional folklore song about Lulu and the dalliances she had. The verses suggest explicit lyrics and it was also popular as a children's schoolyard or bus-trip song. The song has been recorded by early Ska musicians like Lloyd Charmers in 1970 and later covered by various pop artists including Goombay Dance Band and Boney M.

So did the teachers let us sing it because it was part of a folk song classic?

Some folk song!

Did anyone but only a meager few of us know what it REALLY meant? Was that why we were getting 'the look' from our parents when we sang it at home?

Chapter 12 - Twisting Your Dignity Away

Bernice Ethylene Crittenden Knight came home from of the hospital one snowy weekend and was attempting yet another bonding moment with her young daughter.. She watched with interest as I danced to the song "Seven Little Girls in the Backseat" in front of the HiFi. She screamed my father to come watch and told him excitedly that I had a really good beat and maybe someday would be a professional dancer.

That was the day a phone call was made to a neighbour and I was put into a ballet class after school. I will never know if that was a mistake but it did stop me from gaining weight for a few years. As with everything else in life I was a misfit from the word 'go'. I had natural rhythm but just hated regimental bar exercises and my creative steps were frowned upon. After not being able to dance a series of skipping steps for part of the Nutcracker Suite I was banished from ever being a Sugar Plum Fairy and sent to the gallows of the Waltzing Flowers.

Every afternoon at 4 pm I danced my heart away while watching American Bandstand and wished I could go "stroll down the avenue" with Dick Clark. One day Clark introduced Chubby Checker and I attempted to twist while my mother did circles in her wheel chair. For the next month my father would recite every accident known to man which was caused by The Twist. By this time I had every move down pat and was ready to try my moves at the Grade 5-8 dance in the Cowansville High School gym. My mother had made me a soft royal blue jersey dress with a fake fur collar and I had on my broken-in Mary Jane shoes ready to go.

The teachers lined up the boys on one side and the girls faced them not knowing who they were going to get as a dance partner. I looked at this tall lanky boy with a tight suit with high water pants and screamed at him,

"Hey you! I hope you know how to dance!"

He nodded and actually looked afraid of me after I yelled at him, which he probably should have been. The Twist music started and the both of us were just like the dancers on American Bandstand. How two people ages 10 and 11 who had never met each other before danced like professionals is beyond me.

After 20 minutes there were just three couples left in the finals and we were one of them. Ten minutes later after some fancy jumps and spins we won the contest and were each awarded a Cadbury's Snack Bar. Billy, being the gentleman he was, carefully put the candy bars in his pocket and we danced the rest of the night away.

Later I found my friend Sheila and asked her how she thought we did. She promptly told me that the reason we probably won was that my fast dance movements kept spinning my skirt around and I was constantly flashing my underpants. She deemed it a hands down "underpants' win. Mortified that the whole school knew I had on pink underpants I found Billy so I could retrieve my prize from his pocket. Because of the heat in the gym those two Snack Bars were now liquid poop in a wrapper and we quickly threw them out.

Two weeks later at a church dance the girls were once again lined up on one side, and the boys on the other side were instructed to choose their partners. Like a rushing tsunami Billy ran half way, dropping to his knees and slid across the floor to my feet. It was now official - I was now Billy's dancing partner.

I don't think boys have any idea what's coming after they give a "shout out" and a wink of the eye to a young girl. Do they honestly know that within 24 hours the female knows every last personal detail and uses it to rope them in like cattle? Every day I used to ride my bike past his father's business in Sweetsburg and then glance up the hill to see if he was outside. Twice a day I would call him and then hang up quickly when he answered the phone. Billy, if you still have doubts where those phone calls were coming from, your gut feeling was right.

As fast as he danced into my life, Billy "Peppermint Twisted" out of it just as quickly. And so for the next two long years the "Campaign for Billy" continued. By this time my mother had died and I had eaten my way up a few sizes from grief. When they announced the first school dance of the year and Grade 7 was allowed to attend I figured the last battle for Billy was going to be fought that night.

When I now think of this "last battle" I shake my head in embarrassment. With the conviction of William Wallace from Braveheart I had it all planned down to the last "T". I was positive I was going to twist Billy back into my life that very night. Sitting in the hairdressers chair that very afternoon I instructed her to keep teasing and spraying my hair up as far as it would go. Gray box pleated skirt that the zipper would no longer go up was topped by a longish great athletic sweatshirt to cover up the safety pins.

As I spotted him in the far corner of the room surrounded by friends I slowly walked across the gym as they announced Ladies Choice. Each step held my foot like glue and drops of sweat trailed me as I saw the look of fear in his eyes. Billy knew what was going to happen and his friends were trying to stifle their laughter. It was inevitable that Orca the Killer Whale with the sticky unmoving hair was going to ask him to dance.

I stood humbly in front of him, smiled and asked if he wanted to dance. He looked down at his feet and mumbled a few kind words of how I must be happy they allowed the younger grades to come. Then there was dead silence and as he spoke the next few words I knew they would echo in my head for days, weeks or maybe even a lifetime. He said in a very polite hushed tone,

"No thank you!"

And with that I ran out of the gym to the downstairs girls' washroom and cried my alcohol based eyeliner off. That was the end of my campaign for the love of one Billy Jones. Had it been puppy love or something else?

Years later as I heard Twist music on a 60's night in some forlorn corner in Sept-Iles it brought everything 360. With no one wanting to dance I just went out by myself in the middle of the dance floor and twisted solo for three songs. Maybe I was never really in love with Billy or was I? Maybe all I really wanted to do was dance.

Editor's note- The name Billy is a fictitious name to protect the innocent.

Chapter 13 - Back To the Future - Who Were Those Masked Men?

No matter how many years you have been out of High School there will always be a few students that you will remember for being different. These aren't the kids that were smart or athletic; it's the kids that walked down their own highway no matter what the consequences.

Dalton Grenier

When I was in Grade 4 we had a student that was a few years older than most of the class. I don't think any of us actually figured out how many extra years he was carrying or ever asked, but Dalton Grenier was a man among men as they say and had his very own set of school rules, which he stuck by no matter what.

Teachers constantly punished him, yet he would not let their words affect him and always had something funny to say in return. Not very many challenged Dalton, except Grade 4 teacher Miss Wells who despite her shortened height was a spitfire. No matter what she threatened; it never fazed him for one second. Dalton may have never become Prime Minister but as Bob Bromby said,

"Dalton was our very own CHS version of The Fonz!"

And none of us will ever forget him.
Ehhhhhhhhhhhhhhhhhhhhh!

Clayton Smith and the High School Dance Bandit

I began a Facebook discussion last week about someone I remembered from the Cowansville High School dances and after all these years I figured he might have been a figment of my imagination. Had it just been someone I remembered from the film "Peggy Sue Got Married" or did this person really exist?

In the original posting I asked if anyone remembered the well dressed young man that looked a little like Roy Orbison that used to frequent the dances. What set him apart from everyone else is that he would ask each girl to dance, and to my recollection not one girl ever accepted his offer. Most people remembered him, but no one knew exactly who he was.

Larry McCrum-I would say it was probably Clayton Smith, as he had the Brylcream in the hair or it could have been Serge Harvey from Farnham as he was the only 25 year-old at the high school dances.

Claudia Allen-We used to call Clayton Smith "Clayty", but there was another guy who was French, that we used to call Gordie Howe as he looked just like him.

Manuel Grieg-Was it Danny Glenday from Farnham as he used to wear black rimmed glasses?

Bob Bromby-Don't think Danny is the Roy Orbits Son we are searching for. Heck I think even David Hawke wore a pair of dark rimmed glasses back then...Hey maybe it's David...Just kidding!

I can remember a guy who would have been described as a Roy O look alike...Think he rode the Farnham bus. Claude _____?

Of course he never asked me to dance. I was on a training course many years later with a guy who looked a bit like Roy O...He did ask me to dance. I didn't like dancing with Roy Orbison lookalikes either, so I declined.

Audrey Bromby-I recall a guy who used to come to the dances, always asking the girls to dance but can't remember his name. He wore black rimmed glasses and was kinda geeky. Sorta felt sorry for the guy, and he may have come from Farnham but not sure.

Barbara Lacroix- I remember him clearly - gave me the creepy crawlies! It was neither Dalton Grenier nor Clayton Smith, and don't ask me where he came from - never went to CHS as far as I can remember. He was French and I don't think he spoke English. But he was always aware of the dances and never gave up asking girl after girl to dance with very, very little luck. As Linda wrote, I also will remember him forever.

Bob Bromby-Who ever the mystery Mr. O. was he must have carried on his "please dance with me" quest for quite a while as I can recall the same guy and I am a few years senior to you girls. Seeing as no one ever actually danced with the poor guy, maybe the gym at CHS was haunted and Roy was merely an apparition.

Jean Beattie-I remember John Smith used to haunt the dances

Carolyn Watt Boileau-I remember that guy and we used to call him Gordie Howe, and as for Clayton all I remember was that he only sang "North to Alaska"

Wayne King-He is my cousin.

Audrey Bromby-Yes, Clayton was always asking the girls to dance and the boys used to get him up on the stage to - sing.

Barbara Lacroix-If you want to see Clayton, he has been sitting on the bench in front of the Anglican Church. Or sometimes he sits in front of the old Banque Nationale playing his guitar. Believe it or not, he is in his 70's now.

Claudia Allen-Clayton Smith is 70! Hard to believe!

Manuel Grieg-One of you girls should have danced with this mystery man- probably would have made his life better!

Linda Knight Seccaspina-I agree Manuel- what was wrong with us?

Bob Bromby-I had never thought about those school dances until I watched Back to the Future back in '85. It was a super movie, and I still watch it when it replays on TV.

Yes Bob Bromby, we rock and rolled out of that era and into another. Where we're going, we don't need roads anymore to quote Marty McFly, but I bet you Dalton Grenier is still on that super highway and if any of you pass Clayton Smith say hello, as I bet he would love to sing you another chorus of "North to Alaska". In reality Clayton has always been a Johnny B. Goode.

P. S- If anyone wants to know who that mysterious man was at the dances Paul Cornoyer has the answer.

Chapter 14 - Mum, Apple Pie and a Whole Lot of Cheese

When we went to school we ate sugar-filled goodies, nuclear coloured food, and lots of what we would now consider to be called mystery meat. Today High School students that eat cafeteria food blog about how bad it is. All of us ended up surviving no matter what was put in front of us, so I asked the former students of CHS what their favourite food was when they went to school.

Audrey Bromby- My first taste of pizza came from...was it Pizzaroma? It was down near Albany Felt.

Larry McCrum- Toasted chicken sandwich at Le patio restaurant across from the High School.

Jean Beattie- My mother made a totally mean macaroni-and-cheese casserole that completely spoiled me from EVER enjoying that Kraft Dinner stuff out of a package!

Bob Bromby- When taking electronics in Montreal back in 67, Kraft Dinner was 11 cents.

Jean Beattie- Now people think they have a REAL bargain if they can get it for 99 cents on sale! (which it is, if you simply compare prices and ignore what's in/not in it)

Linda Mewett- My moms cooking in general, she is the best cook! But to choose I have to say Roast Beef Sunday dinner with Yorkshire Pudding and gravy plus veggies ummmm!!!! I have to add, French fries and sauce at Harry's then the fresh donuts at the pastry shop.

Margaret Clay Jacob- Since we didn't go out to the restaurant as a family back in the day my favorite after the movies or a school dance was a Club Sandwich at Don's Restaurant beside the theatre.

Kelly Reagan- Remember how much better all food tasted before the "cholesterol" paranoia got started?! I know it spoiled a lot of my fun. Yeah, the good ol' days!

Audrey Bromby- We even used to drink whole milk straight from the cow on the farm. Best milk I ever had.

Audrey Bromby- In the winter, we had roast beef, mashed potatoes and gravy at home and in the summer my father would get a chicken from the chicken coop and we'd have fresh plucked roast chicken for dinner. Except back then "dinner" was at lunchtime.

Kelly Reagan- Drinking whole milk made me remember the cream at the top of the milk bottle. A dollop of whipped cream over the top of mother's apple pie...yuuuummmmmm!

Audrey Bromby- Ohhh Kelly...you are making me drool! Nothing better than that homemade whipped cream and apple pie.

Manuel Greig @ Audrey Bromby..."Old" cheese and apple pie !!!!

Audrey Bromby- Now you've done it Manuel Greig..I just put on 10 lbs. lol

Kelly Reagan- What was that old saying?...apple pie without the cheese is like a hug without a squeeze! Well, all that good food and here we all are, we survived the cholesterol and lived to tell about it! I also remember my grandmothers homemade bread spread thick with butter she churned herself! ;o ...I'm making myself hungry!

David Hawke- Can you still get good old cheddar in Quebec? It's almost impossible on Ontario & impossible here.

Manuel Greig - David Hawke...Ya, you can get "Sharp" and "Extra Sharp" here...

Audrey Bromby- But it just doesn't taste the same as in the ole days.

Claudia Forster Allen-Other than Harry's you couldn't beat my mothers roast turkey, stuffing and all the trimmings, mashed potatoes, hubbard squash and parsnips/carrots and gravy tons and tons of gravy. . stuffing and turkey sandwiches with gravy for supper, as if you weren't stuffed enough . . . apple pie, pumpkin pie with lots of whipped cream straight from the milk tin . . all the Taylor clan together at Christmas with lots of laughter, jokes, wild tales and noise! Lots and lots of noise. sigh, I miss that!

Audrey Bromby- Oh good gawwwd...all this talk of home cooking and great food...I'm going to make a sandwich!

David Hawke- Have to pick some up, do like 5-7 yr old cheddar.

David Hawke- Cook's making supper as I write this.

Claudia Forster Allen- Make one for me too, k? Audrey? yes, love a sandwich and a cuppa tea . . oh and make a loaf to bring to the "Gathering" while yer at it, K? Thanks ♥

Manuel Greig- At Christmas, for dessert we had Christmas pudding with hard sauce.....Yummy !!!!

Manuel Greig -@ Audrey Bromby-I'll have the same as Claudia, please, since you're making it.

Claudia Forster Allen- I had a Boom Burger and poutine from Boom Burger here on the Prince Edward Island. Using island made cheese. Very yummy and the gravy was pretty darn good. Actually it was a Boom Grilled Cheese with grilled onions, mushrooms, tomatoes, bacon and mayo. Then I hopped into the car and headed to the beach for a swim. Marvelous end to a long hot day. . raining now...

Audrey Bromby- I was about the only one in my family who loved that Christmas pudding and sauce. *sigh* I want my Mommy!!!

Claudia Forster Allen - Mom didn't like raisins so we never got that she would make the sauce and put it on something else, probably gingerbread . . lol I didn't eat plum pudding till I went to Ireland and ate my cousins. . Wow have I missed out. . . lol

Audrey Bromby- You still want a sandwich after pigging out at Boom Burger Claudia!?!?! Oink Oink!

Claudia Forster Allen- hahahaha, the swim evened it out...hahahahahaha

Audrey Bromby- All that delicious baking at Christmas. Mom used to make all sorts of pies, squares etc.

Audrey Bromby- Group cry..Group cry....*sigh*

Jeffrey Bromby- My first pizza was at the Roma in Cowansville.....near Albany Felt. Pizza was a new thing and everyone was thin and in shape. Those damn Italians !! Gotta be their fault!! Bless the Pizza. I'd eat it 7 days a week and wash it down with beer!!

Claudia Forster Allen- I remember that place we always went there after a night of drinking . . . lol best pizza in town . .

Claudia Forster Allen- I was in love with a red-head in those days . . :) lol

Jeffrey Bromby- Pizza is also great for breakfast.

Manuel Greig @Claudia Forster Allen...who was the red-head ?????

Audrey Bromby- Do tell Ms Claudia!

Manuel Greig- Ya you too Audrey Bromby...from a post last night !!!

Claudia Forster Allen- You tell first, Audrey . . you know, the one from Knowlton.

Audrey Bromby- With all this food I've had tonight...Christmas dinners, roast beef, roast chicken, pie, Harry's french fries and sauce, pizza, Christmas pudding....*yawn*...I need a nap (And NO I'm not telling. Besides, you don't know him :p~~~~~~~)

Claudia Forster Allen- does that mean your lips are sealed? :(

Linda Knight Seccaspina- If you aren't going to spill da beans - spill da pie!

Editor's Note – A Story of Apple Pie and Whipped Cream from Charne Tromp

She saw him from across the room, sipping slowly on his freshly brewed cup of nothing, trying his best to go unnoticed and fill the emptiness inside of him with his cup of nothingness. He'd been coming there for months, at first alone, just to people watch, with nothing more than a book to keep him company. He'd had a certain quiet confidence about him, always friendly, but not big on conversation. What had stood out about him was his kind eyes and his gentle manner.

She had tried many times to pry into the pages of his very private demeanor, while serving him his regular warm brew with a fry up, but all she ever got in return to her questioning looks was a polite 'thank you'. She knew how he liked his coffee, knew that he liked his eggs sunny-side-up and that he always asked for extra cream with his Apple pie.

Then one glorious Summer day he had showed up for his regular breakfast, but this time he was not alone. He was accompanied by a beautiful brunette with scarlet lips and a overwhelming laughter. He ordered his regular, while she placed an order for a skinny latte and some fresh whole-wheat crumpets. They sat there, the two of them, the picture of young love, all giddy and brimming over with happiness and all the while she would talk and he would nod and listen.

They kept coming back together for weeks and weeks until the trees had been stripped bare of all their leaves and the air grew chilly. One grey morning he came in for his usual accompanied by loneliness and heartache. He ordered his regular and sat by the window. The people on the street were of no interest to him, neither was the book resting on the table beside him.

She noticed he'd lost a bit of his light and his eyes no longer shone as brightly. On this particular day though, she had no need to pry as to the reason for his lack of luster. She, who was never at a loss for words, on this particular day could not find the words. So instead she served him his regular fry up with a cup of brew and watched him move his food around his plate. Once she'd cleared away his barely eaten breakfast, she brought him his Apple Pie with three extra helpings of cream, because sometimes there are no words and all you have to give is whipped cream

Chapter 15 - "The One About Disappearing Friends"

My childhood friend Sheila Wallet kept every letter and piece of paper that I had ever sent to her from 1973-1989. Sheila emailed me last year and asked me if I wanted all the old letters and newspaper clippings I had sent her throughout the years. When I received them they were neatly piled and carefully dated with the envelopes stapled to the letters. I had never seen anything like it and questioned whether my friend had OCD or was just efficient.

Sheila had always been the loyal friend that I waited for every morning, at approximately 8:35 on Albert Street, to walk to school. She had experienced most of my life first hand and was one of the very few friends who turned up at my father's funeral in Quebec. We have not seen each other in years, but deep down we both know that the other is still there and both of us still value and cherish our friendship.

So this week's question was:

If you could meet up once again with a few former classmates not on this Facebook group, who would it be?

Pennie Redmile- For me - it would be Dawn Burnley. I would dearly love to hear news of her.

Margaret Clay Jacob- My wish would be to see my old friend Christine Jadeck who I have not seen for close to 48 yrs.

Manuel Greig @ Margaret-I don't know about Christine, but her sister, Alina, lives in Sutton.

Margaret Clay Jacob- Manuel, do you know Alina's married name? I would love to contact her.

Manuel Greig @ Margaret-No, but I could find out for you!

Margaret Clay Jacob- Thanking you in advance.

David Hawke- Jerry Kokitko, Claire Crawford, Nadine Rouse

Manuel Greig- Joan Longtin, Glenda Chan

Linda Knight Seccaspina- Leslye and Nelson Wyatt, and Debby Roffey. I would also like to personally apologize to Jimmy Manson and Butch McElroy for my actions 48 years ago.

Bob Bromby @Linda..Can't do anything about Leslye, Nelson or Jimmy....but Butch will be paying us a visit in Carp on Canada Day.

Linda Knight Seccaspina- Bob- please extend my apologies!

Editor's Note- Dinner and a Movie With Bob Bromby follows:

Bob Bromby- As for former classmates to meet up with and have dinner with-any of the cheerleading groups would suit me fine.

Kelly Reagan- Bob, you want to meet up with some of the cheerleaders? Don't forget, bodies change A LOT...after all these years. Just sayin'...;o

Bob Bromby- Kelly, Cheerleaders never age. I had a dream last night that had a CHS cheerleader in it...She hadn't aged a day since 1964...:)))

Kelly Reagan- Ha,ha...gives credence to the saying..."only in your dreams". Hey, you know...whatever makes you happy.

John Farrell- I hung out with the same group for the last couple of years in high school here's my pick from them.

The guy...Butch McElroy

And for the gal...Louise Chatham

Bob Bromby- If I could meet up with a few former classmates... Norm Wilson, Stan Aiken, Dennis McCulloch, Paul Jordan, Bill Joa to name a few...RIP Guys.

Audrey Bromby- I'm with Linda in choosing Leslye & Nelson Wyatt. I spent a lot of time at their house in my teens getting into mischief and many a weekend at the Wyatt house. We would get home from a night out and Nelson would be there waiting for us. We used to draw straws to see who would go over to the Gai Canton to get food. I would also like to see Florence Elms again. We were good friends in grade school and she took the same school bus as I did. I have seen her a few times but not in a long while.

Manuel Greig @ Audrey- You got into mischief?? No..Unbelievable !!!

Audrey Bromby@ Manuel Greig- Who?? moi??? mischief? nevvvva!

Carolyn Watt Boileau Linda & Audrey- If you want to see Leslye, she is at the Legion every year for Remembrance Day ceremony laying a wreath in her father's honour. Nelson was also there last year.

Linda Knight Seccaspina @ Audrey... We ate the Gai Canton on River Street out of fried rice.:) I think we thought it was some medieval diet food.

Audrey Bromby- Yup, ole Bill Wong saw us coming lol!

Claudia Forster Allen- I would like to see all of them!

Audrey Bromby- I would also like to add Richard Bilow, Peter Bodanaw (sp) and John Sloergeris. We used to meet up at the Patio after school.

Editor's Note: Le Patio- "les patates avec sauce s'il vous plait!" - nurse that dish with the smallest glass of Pepsi you have ever seen for about 3 hours.

Claudia Forster Allen- Maybe we should have a walking tour of the "downtown" area and reminisce about the places that USED to be there sometime.

Audrey Bromby- Unfortunately most of the old haunts are no longer there *sigh*

Claudia Forster Allen- I know, boooooo, we could visualize tho . . lol, stand around in a group and point, laugh and giggle . . :)

Audrey Bromby- Do we really wanna let lose in downtown Cowansville?!?! lol They wouldn't know what hit 'em!

Audrey Bromby- We could sit on a bench where Harry's used to be and eat french fries.

David Hawke- It was bad enough when Crappy Tire was still in the hole or somewhere thereabouts, can imagine it's a disaster now and I would just as soon leave well enough alone.

Audrey Bromby- Actually they've tried to spruce up the downtown area. No more Harry's and Continental and it's all replaced by a nice park area. No more Ritz or Arsenault's shoe store. The hotel has been renovated and is now a residence for Alzheimer's patients. The Princess Theatre is still there.

Bob Bromby- If we all congregated in the park where Harrys used to be, the only thing missing (other than the pool room) would be the town police cops insisting that we "circulez..circulez"! They used to threaten us with arrest for loitering when we hung out in front or sat on the fence between Harrys.

Claudia Forster Allen- I remember! I do believe some people would stand up and turn in circles and I can't remember who . . :)

Audrey Bromby- I believe that was Leon Pearcy.

Claudia Forster Allen- Now there's a name I haven't heard in a very long time.

Margaret Clay Jacob@ David Hawke- Two of your choices of people to see again are right around here. Jerry has retired from I.B.M. and Nadine is also still here. She married Marcel Lachance (an ex policeman) then they had an ice cream parlour but sold it a couple of years ago. Claire (my cousin) left for Ontario a couple of years after she got married and is still there, in London, I believe. If I can do anything to help you contact Jerry and Nadine for the Labour Day weekend, let me know.

David Hawke-Thanks Margaret actually I did hunt Jerry up when I was down four years ago and will do so this time but it would be nice if you could contact Nadine. Good times were had in East Farnham back in the day, I remember her mom's Austin cool little car.

Audrey Bromby@ Margaret- Aren't you related to Florence Elms? If so, do you know if she has an email address or can you give me her home address?

Margaret Clay Jacob- Audrey, I really don't know if Florence has an email address but I do have her telephone number and address.

David Hawke- Margaret, actually I did hunt Jerry up when I was down four years ago and will do so this time but it would be nice if you could contact Nadine. Good times were had in East Farnham back in the day, I remember her mom's Austin cool little car.

Audrey Bromby- I just had a nice phone conversation with my old friend, Florence Elms (thanks to Margaret Clay Jacob).She doesn't have a computer and has no desire to get one. She says she's too old to learn new tricks and it sure was nice to talk to her.

Claudia Forster Allen- I remember Florence well, Audrey . . next time you speak to her tell her I said hello.

Epilogue:

My friend Sheila and I both tried to make a difference to people in our lives. Who knew when we first became friends at the age of 2, what our destiny would be like. But if I die tomorrow I know that I have tried-just like Sheila.

I'll be there for her always in spirit just like everyone else on our CHS Facebook group and the friends you have not seen in years- as after all-

That's what friends are for!

Chapter 16 - Rattling Your Pies in the Sky

I asked the former students of CHS on Facebook what unique gifts they have offered the world and what their present passion was. Responses were slow because we are now in the heat of summer vacation; so I have decided to put it all into a melting pot of thoughts this week.

Last year I read a blog about "rattling pies in the sky" by a friend named Kit Duncan and was confused because I had never heard that term before. Being Canadian I have heard of a "pie in the sky", but no where had I heard of pies being rattled. I sat there after reading her post and wondered how much pie rattling I really had accomplished.

When I was 14, because of my theatrical flare of dressing, people told me I should become a fashion designer. My father could not deal with those specific "pies" and the constant conversation of my dreams to him were ignored. He found me "flighty" and way too creative for anyone's good, and when I was having trouble in school he strongly suggested a stint in the Canadian Army, like he had done.

My grandfather, concerned about not losing the "creative child" as he called me, insisted I be sent to England to the London School of Design. It was 1967, and I had dreams of

Carnaby Street, the Beatles and fashion. My father was not amused and he wanted my pies in the sky kept at home and preferably on Canadian soil. Long story short, my grandfather died in early August of that year and any promise of schooling in the UK came to a screeching halt. After a lot of arguing I left home and attended fashion design school in Montreal.

Was it the right pie in the sky?

I think so.

I worked very hard and opened my own business at age 24. From 1974-1997, I owned a couple of clothing stores that made an impact on the Ottawa Valley locals. Through my clothing designs I let people become who they wanted to be through fashion. I applauded their acceptance of being themselves, and told them that being different was okay. Watching my shoppers grow up and having their children come into my stores was amazing. First and foremost; it was always important to me to always be there for those who needed to talk and for those who felt the pressures of being unique.

Reuniting with my former classmates from CHS on Facebook has been the greatest gift that has been handed to me. All of you became parts of my pie in the sky and there is not one day that does not go by that I do not thank my lucky stars.

So how did the former students of CHS rattle their pies?

Keith McClatchie - My teaching management skills, acting and singing. Now that I'm retired, my goal is to be able to play the guitar.

David Hawke- Had a blast teaming up with an assortment of unique individuals to tilt windmills while thumbing my nose at the establishment to provide excellent transportation service to my clients. Now living the quiet life (sort of) in the tropics.

Sheila Perry- Nursing-helping young Mom's with their newborns-and Palliative Nursing care, of which I'm still doing! Being a Mom and Grandmother.

Jean Beattie- Nothing very unique--people have commented over the years on my pleasant voice on the telephone, and my tact... Neither is unique to me :) My current interests are friends, painting (canvasses, not walls) and the various things involving the computer--social contacts, games, various programs and their uses... and my cat. The order varies :D lol

Audrey Bromby- I haven't gotten there yet lol

Claudia Forster Allen- My passion has always been helping people in whatever capacity, organizing, baking, volunteering for Meals on Wheels, functions for fund raisers . . . achieving my passion after many years . . making chocolates and using my culinary skills. . got a need? just ask me. :)

Audrey Bromby- As ole blue eyes sang....I've lived a life that's full.

I traveled each and ev'ry highway.

And more, much more than this, I did it my way

Regrets, I've had a few

But then again, too few to mention.

Claudia Forster Allen- I hummed this dang song all day today, Audrey! lol

Audrey Bromby- Doncha hate when that happens?! lol

Claudia Forster Allen- Yes, yes I do . . haha

Bob Bromby- Unique gift.....hmmmm! Used to be a cracker jack computer fixer, until the darn things got shrunk and got smarter than me..Current passion...seeking out songs recorded in the last 20 years that are worth listening to.

Claudia Forster Allen- My passion at this moment is being the best dang "hooker" around . . . rug hooker that is . . . . .

Bob Bromby- Nuttin' tops a passionate hooker who can also bake a boysenberry pie.

Claudia Forster Allen- Boysenberry or poisonberry??? . .. lol

Editor's Note- Food Network's Paula Deen says everyone can have a piece of pie in moderation. I think we all realized that.

Chapter 17 - School Spirit and Thoughts from Early and Late Bloomers

This week the 1973 film American Graffiti was brought up in conversation and I decided to ask everyone where they were in the year of '62. Most of us on the Facebook board were still hitting the candy stores in those days but there are older 60's teenagers in our group and we wanted to know what Cowansville's very own Curt Henderson and Steve Bolander were up to.

David Hawke - In '62 I was chomping at the bit waiting for my 17th birthday, the magic day, when I could finally take my drivers test. Spent the '61/'62 school year at Feller College boarding school (an excellent adventure) to avoid being in the class of a teacher I couldn't stand. The following year came wheels and drive-ins across the Vermont border. It wasn't until a couple years later while pipe lining in Belleville ON that I first experienced "cruisin' the main drag" (American Graffiti style), A & W Drive-in restaurants and going down to the Bay to watch the submarine races!

Linda Knight Seccaspina (who always comments on food)- I can smell the Teen Burgers from here David!

With all the conversation of the early 60's Sheila Perry posted an interesting article from a vintage CHS annual The Hylite.

Last Will and Testament of the Graduating Class of 1964

We, the graduating class of 1964, being of sound (?) mind and bruised bodies, do, this the 11th days of the month of May 1964 bequeath the following to the future Grade XI class in hopes that they will benefit there-from.

I, Agnes-Jane Greig, bequeath to Christine Jadack my chemistry notes which are high-lighted with hockey players' pictures between the pages.

I, Christina Pratt, leave to Carol Longtin my basketball shorts and running shoes with which to lead the Senior Girls' Basketball team on to victory next year.

I, Doreen Mekety, will to Mike Ellis my ability to try and convince Mr. Douglas that the "Canadiens" are still the BEST.

I, Roger Corey, bequeath to Randy Wood my ability to predict Stanley Cup winners, namely-Toronto.

I, Billy Longtin, leave to Carole Ferris my slightly incomplete geometry notes in hopes that she may have better luck in understanding them than I.

I, David Hawke bequeath my Hot Rod Magazines to Bob Bromby so he could read them during literature class.

David Hawke- Many forgotten memories here

Bob Bromby @David-.So where are MY Hot Rod mags?

David Hawke- Didn't you get them? I left them on the counter at the back of the room and I think there was a Honest Charlies catalog there also.

Larry McCrum- I was only 10 in 1962 but remember it as the Cuban missile crisis and preparations for nuclear attack! Here's some other things I looked up:

The Cost of Living in 1962

Yearly Inflation Rate USA 1.20%

Yearly Inflation Rate UK 3.6%

Year End Close Dow Jones Industrial Average 652

Average Cost of new house $12,500.00

Average Income per year $5,556.00

Average monthly rent $110.00 per month

Tuition to Harvard University $1,520.00

All Wheel Drive Scout off road $2,150.00

Renault Imported car $1,395.00

Average Cost of a new car $3,125.00

Eggs per dozen 32 cents

Gas per Gallon 28 cents

Factory Workers Average Take Home Pay with 3 dependents $94.87

Claudia Allen- We had no clue Larry. We were still wet behind the ears!

Audrey Bromby- Wow, I was still a wee girl of 12 with a twinkle in my eye and mischief in my thoughts. I was riding my bike and hanging around with my friends. Going swimming at the old swimming hole not far from my house.

Claudia Allen- '62, yikes, that's is actually my age NOW . I can remember sitting at the Bluebird Restaurant having egg rolls and coke and listening to the juke box . We were too young for Harry's Poolroom then.

Barbara Lacroix- The Bluebird - everyone went after seeing 2 movies for 50 cents (or was it 25 cents) -the best Chinese food ever!

David Hawke- So when did Harry's open? I know we went north from the school to Frank's Pool Room most of my high school years, only remember going to Harry's the last year, maybe 2.

Since we began the CHS Facebook group Harry's Poolroom on South Street seems to be a beloved and greatly missed part of our lives. Harry's was American Graffiti's Mel's Restaurant to everyone that went to Cowansville High School. One might think that if they ever create a CHS museum it should be built on the site of Harry's.

Audrey Bromby - How many of you skipped school every now and then? My friend Joan and I skipped an afternoon and headed to Harry's Pool Room and helped Kenny Taylor peel potatoes. Who came strolling up the street- the good Reverend Peacock. Kenny told us to hide in the poolroom until he left. That was one lonnng cup of coffee!

From Harry's the discussion literally went from the top to bottom and was grabbed by the early bloomers as they posted about their bottoms. Well- cheerleading bloomers anyways.

Claudia Allen-Anyone remember the Cowansville High School Cheers?

Audrey Bromby- 2-4-6-8 who do we appreciate (enter name of player) Yay team!

Audrey Bromby- Let's go let's go let's really go...let's fight let's fight..lets really fight!

Audrey Bromby- How corny!! lol

Claudia Allen- It wasn't corny then .. . and now it's more than a hoot!

Kelly Reagan- You're right, it wasn't corny or hokey then, we were just a bunch of kids having fun together

Claudia Allen- Yup it was fun . . and look here we are talking about it and singing and carrying on just like then . . .

David Hawke- It's called school spirit and the team supporters on the bus had to pay a quarter to ride. Good times those sports trips.

Kelly Reagan- A memory becomes great when you can share it with others. That is why this Facebook site is great, because we all remember bits and pieces of the same big picture.

Barbara Lacroix- When you're up, you're up, when you're down, you're down, when you're up against Cowansville, you're upside down (and that's when Amy & I would do our cartwheels), razzle, dazzle, sis boom bah, Cowansville High School, rah, rah, rah!

Claudia Allen- I remember that one Barb!

Claudia Allen- There was no itty bitty teeny weeny bikini underwear for us in those days. I know the skirt was a white top of some kind..maybe someone else will recall those wonderful happy days!!! We all thought we were great!!!

Claudia- All of you were great but you just ever realized it at that age. But to quote the film American Graffiti:

We just couldn't stay seventeen forever!

Cowansville High School Misremembered

What happened?

Thoughts?

Clues?

Anyone got a time machine?

Never mind, we will be forever young!

Chapter 18 - More Dances, More Music and the French Gals

Unless you lived under some rock on Sutton Mountain most of the CHS kids will remember the square dances at the old school house in East Farnham and the monthly dance at the High School gym. Not to remain in the shadows were Reverend Peacock's dances at the Anglican church hall, and the Knights of Columbus Hall's live band teen extravaganzas. Barbara Lacroix remembers hanging out in the church hall learning to square dance on a Friday night with Ron Browning as her partner, but there seemed to be other places that I had never even heard of.

Noreen Duross-Anyone remember the Chickwick (sp?) at Brome Lake?

Claudia Allen-Did that become the Terrace? I remember the name!

Editor's Note- Claudia- please see Cowansville High School- Hippies, Pasties and the Tear-Azz Bar for reference.:)

Noreen Duross-No, it was where the Joli Vent is now. It was a barn-like building behind the main building. The Terrace was in Bondville; whereas this was on the road towards Foster and Highway 10. They played a lot of rock and roll records like Rock around the Clock and songs of the Bill Haley and the Comets era. Probably way before your time and that of most of the people "chatting" here!

Keith McClatchie-I remember the Chickwick very well, how about Stone's Hotel up in West Shefford? (Now Bromont) It is still there. or the Brome Lake Manoir? It burnt to the ground a lot of years ago.

Maureen Forster Page-I remember school dances, church dances, Christophe Columbe dances, and the one below the bowling alley. Went to a few at Selby Lake in summer and a camp site somewhere between Cowansville and Farnham. I remember some St. Leon boys coming to our dances. Never went to The Terrasse Inn after hearing of a raid there.

Editor's Note-I remember the St. Leon boys coming to our dances and after that tidbit strange subjects began to surface. According to David Hawke there were also dances at St. Leon and he was quick to point out that you could actually try out some of that French you were taught in our beloved Mrs. Blinn's class. Oh, if we could get footage of those blessed moments with our fair CHS boys conversing with " les francoises".

Audrey Bromby-I went to a couple at St. Leon and the priests circled the dance floor making sure nobody was dancing too close together lol.

Editor's Note-And were you Audrey??:)

Barbara Lacroix-There were actually dances at St Leon school??? Never went there!!

Linda Knight Seccaspina-Me either Barbara- someone was holding out!

David Hawke- It was a whole new set of girls at St. Leon dances, after the same same at CHS!

Manuel Greig@ Barbara- I didn't go to many dances....and the French girls were friendly!

Linda Knight Seccaspina- Well I hear some of the french guys were friendlier too!

Claudia Allen-Don't touch dat!

Barbara Lacroix-O.K. - French girls friendlier!!???? In what way??

Manuel Greig-I just said they were friendly......

Barbara Lacroix-And the English ones weren't!!!!

Roberta R Barnes-hahahaah

Manuel Greig-Some of them were, I guess !!!! Some were snarky too !!!

I wonder what happened to their sense of humour ????

Barbara Lacroix-Manuel - you're lucky that we "English" girls didn't know this about the "French" girls when we were in school with you!!!! You would have been skating on very thin ice!!!

Editor's Note-Readers- please notice the amount of exclamation marks Barbara and Manuel used!

Manuel Grieg-As I saw it, the ice wasn't very thick then...and like I said,"......." !!!

Audrey Bromby-Looks like you've stepped into a bit of doggie do-do Manuel..lol

David Hawke-You're on your own now Manuel, those English girls are getting persnickety.

Bob Bromby-Manuel..you are learning to "dance".... quickly :-)

Keep dancing Manuel...a moving target is harder to hit.

Manuel Greig- Wanna go fishing?? looks like I've opened a can of worms...

Editor's Note- The late Huzon Grenier then reminded us (or cleverly changed a hot subject) that Smiley Willette played Plattsburgh WPTZ and that Smokey Smith and Terry Sutton played with them for awhile. Total silence grabbed the group until the next question:

What was your favourite song in school?

David Hawke-The only one I could really dance to, The Bunny Hoppppp!

For snuggle dancin---Bobby Vinton's "Blue Velvet"

A couple instrumentals Harbor Lights, Wheels From Breakfast at Tiffany's "Moon River" "Four Strong Winds" Ian & Sylvia Sheb Wooley's one eyed one horned flying purple eater Hound Dog + a whole bunch of good stuff by the Pelvis "Rocky Mountain High" "Leaving on a Jet Plane" John Denver

Linda Knight Seccaspina-Sounds like David can really move!

Jean Beattie-Appluase and more applause!

Bob Bromby- "Twist n Shout" (fast) ..."Smoke gets in your eyes" (snuggle dancin')

Carole Beattie- "The Twist" (Chubby Checker)..... "Unchained Melody" (snuggle dancin') "Love Me Tender" (Elvis)......."I'm Sorry" (Brenda Lee) 'Time In A Bottle". 'Surf City' (The Beach Boys)

"I Wanna Hold Your Hand" (The Beatles)

"Wake Up A-Little Suzie... Wake Up" (The Everly Brothers)

Paul Cournoyer - Young Love by Sonny James.

Manuel Grieg- "Unchained Melody", " Have You Ever Really Loved a Woman" Louie Louie .... Crystal Chandeliers" (Charlie Pride)..."Down in the Boondocks"(Billy Joe Royal) "The Sounds of Silence"(Simon and Garfunkel) Me and Bobby McGee"(Janis Joplin) , Linda Ronstadt, Johnny Cash, Marty Robbins...Neil Diamond.. The Four Season's..."Walk Like a Man" I Love a Rainy Night"...Eddie Rabbitt

Bridge Over Troubled Water...(Simon & Garfunkel Start Me Up....(Rolling Stones) "The Wanderer"..(Dion and the

Belmonts)..."Leader of the Pack"..(Shangrai-Las) Cher I Think I Love You...(The Partridge Family)

Claudia Allen So what am I so afraid of . . . . :))

Linda Knight Seccaspina- That they will keep adding to this darn list!

Editor's Note: They never stopped and then got "all Grade 1" on me and asked why there was no Beach Boy list:

A Special Tribute to The Beach Boys

Carole Beattie "Surf City" !!!!

Claudia Allen- Little GTO

Audrey Bromby -Surfer Girl (cuddle song)

Manuel Grieg- Good Vibrations....:o) "Kokomo"

David Hawke- Shut Down, Little Deuce Coup, Little GTO, Chevy 409

Editor's List-HOLD THE PHONE! Bob Bromby says we are not done yet!

Bob Bromby-Whoa!....List ain't complete without 'Deadmans Curve'.....Jan & Dean..."cruisin in my Stingray late on nite.....

Cowansville High School Misremembered

Editor's Note- And that's a wrap folks!

Chapter 19 - Hippies, Pasties and the "Tear-Azz" Bar

One morning last week I woke up and had memories of my teenage years as a weekend hippie. No one in the Knight family could be a full time one according to my father; so I did my best with the limited time I was allowed.

I remember one day in 1966 sitting at the Riviera Cafe/Harry's Poolroom with my friends at lunchtime and hearing The Buffalo Springfield's new song For What it's Worth. Everybody in that cafe instantly came together and sang the song at full volume until each note was over.

Were there really Hippies at Cowansville High School and who were they? No one can really recall that many except that Audrey Bromby said Robert Forster did wear his hair long but she could never picture him as a hippie. And what is up with Gordie Leonard?

There were also rumours running rampant of a certain High School teacher being fired as he used to invite some of the students to his house and give them LSD! Didn't they make B-movies on this subject or did the certain teacher end up being in one?

Being a budding hippie I idolized fellow student Joan Longtin who used to come into our classroom at recess and play "The House of the Rising Sun" on her guitar. To me, she was Cowansville High School's Joan Baez. When I mentioned Longtin on the CHS Facebook board everyone remembered and wondered what happened to her.

Jean Beattie thought that Pat Fontaine, who taught at at Massey Vanier, was Joan's son but Nancy Hamm didn't agree. Ms. Hamm said that Pat Fontaine was Carol Longtin's son which would be Joan's nephew. Joan, as far as Nancy knew was not married and living out west. No one else on the board had a clue what she might be up to and but all recalled how talented she was.

Audrey remembered when Leslye Wyatt and I wore bellbottoms and mine were from Eaton's and made out of a heavy backed green acrylic fabric that made me look exactly like Gumby. Manuel Grieg thought mini skirts were a lot better and the thread on the world of hippies vanished and turned into a subject that I had no idea was coming.

From the innocent talk of Friday night dances when the boys used to get up on stage and lip-sync while playing their hockey stick's; it was on to talk of the impressive guitar strains of Des King and Alan Webb. Suddenly the conversation turned 360.

Bob Bromby-Speaking of watering holes. What was the name of the place that was popular late 60's at Bondville? Can remember they checked ID to try to curb underage when a 'raid' was due. Remember Bob Mc sneaking in through the bathroom window and I think Joe Cocker wrote a song about it.

Linda Knight Seccaspina-Joe Cocker wrote a song about an Eastern Townships watering hole?

Audrey Bromby-It was the Terrace (Tear-Azz) Inn.

David Hawke-Didn't they have the first go-go girls in the area dancing in cages above the floor?

Bob Bromby-I don't recall go-go girls at the Tear-Azz, at least while I was a Saturday night visitor. The Riverview in Bedford was a hot spot for us underage crowd before the Tear-Ass. The Beach Boys song Baa Baa Baa, Baa Barbara Ann played by the live band whose singer was called" Humma " who hailed from Farnham.

Claudia Allen-Cages I seem to remember but they didn't last. Must be a biker gang owned it for awhile.

David Hawke - 'twas the Tear-azz that had the dancin' gals in the oversized bird cages, gosh danged know 'twas!!!---- yep we did travel for a party!

Bob Bromby-There were GO-GO Girls at Gilmore's Inn after it converted from C&W around 1970 give or take. Cages too and pasties to boot.....or did you say pastries.......Aaaah!.....drool! The Tear Azz was a rock n roll hoochie coo kinda spot whenever I was there. Not a go-go girl in sight and the only cage I ever saw there was a pig crate they used to transport me there for my stag party which got plopped into the lake leaving me just enough head room to breath. With friends like that I didn't need enemies.Thanks Carters, McKells, Moreton, Royea and all....Glad you had fun...'cause I sure didn't......Still lookin' to get even!

Bob Bromby-My education in those matters (Chesty Morgan) are deficient also.....wink...wink. Saw her perform once...can't remember where. Don't think it was Gilmores though....just recall the performance....a very 'big' artistic presentation if memory serves me right...wink...wink.

And finally our voice of reason Jean Beattie summed it all up for us:

Jean Beattie-My education is deficient in these matters, but I remember that, before Gilman's closed, there was an ad for Chesty Morgan who must have been rather aged by that time as her pasties drooped down to "here" in the photo that accompanied the ad!

And like an episode of Masterpiece Theatre we ended this CHS episode by saying that Chesty Morgan stopped performing in the 80's, and we all know what happened to her by searching on Wikipedia. Alas, whatever happened to guitar-player Joan Longtin from Cowansville High School will forever remain a mystery.

Footnote:

The Terrace (Tear-Azz) was in Bondville (Brome Lake) and Gilmore's was at Gilman's Corner where the road to Sutton and Knowlton/Cowansville, Quebec intersect.

Larry McCrum (Our resident Wikipedia)

Chapter 20 - Fire Drills, Loud Bells and a Whole Lot of Noise

Judith Bell wrote this week on the Cowansville High School Facebook group that the Massey Vanier School Board had installed a new phone system last August and the bells had just started functioning six weeks ago. Memories flooded my mind remembering our beloved fire drills and the crazy bell system we used to have at CHS.

As Claudia Allen remembers; the bells were so loud they could be heard as far as Harry's Pool Room on South Street, which was just a skip and a jump over the Yamaska River. That must have been such a bonus for all those playing pool during the lunch hour!

Of course that first bell in the morning was five minutes before 9 and you had to run like heck to get to the new section in the basement playrooms.

According to Bob Bromby; Mr. Douglas (who seemed like he was 7 ft 2 in those days) slowly did his inspection between the rows like a drill sergeant. I swear if you took a breath Mr. Douglas might flash that evil eye, or finger point a detention.

I agree with Claudia Allen that the absolute worst was Miss Parsons, who would not think twice in sending you to the office. If I remember correctly there were always at least a half a dozen bodies sitting by the office as we marched up to our classrooms waiting to see the Principal.

When I started school in the late 50's the strap was still legal and at least once a week we would hear the same three brothers getting their hands slapped in the office for being late. It seemed almost like an opera with one crying out first and then the other two joining in unison. Pavarotti they were not!

David Hawke says he doesn't remember any forced lineups until he hit Grade 8 on the second floor of the original section. But he and the rest of us remember the fire drills like it was yesterday.

Jean Beattie agreed no one was ever silent during those drills, even though those teachers tried their best! Arms must be folded, and one person was chosen to give up their life, check the classrooms and make sure everyone was out of the building.

If it had been a real fire according to Claudia Allen, whoever had been hauled out of line and made to stand facing the wall for talking probably would have ended up being fried-chicken.

Like Audrey Bromby said; once we were all in line and quiet you could hear the "click click click" of Grade 2 teacher's Miss Spicer's high heels coming down the hall.

"Aaaah!....Miss Spicers high heels....drool", the former male students chorused together on Facebook.

In your wildest dreams boys!!

But that folks is another story!

Chapter 21 - Our Miss Phelps

Sitting in a grade 9 art class I wondered how I could do a book cover art project and relate it to the latest "infatuation" in my life. I cannot remember how the word eagle came in to play right now and wonder if it might have been the imaginary boyfriend's nickname. But there I was showing art teacher Miss Marion Phelps my idea of doing a cover for a book called "The Eagle Has Landed".

She stood back and lowered her glasses a tad and then gave me a small pat on the back. Quite perplexed; she asked me why on earth I was going to do something like that when others in the class were doing book covers of popular subjects. Of course she was completely right and had she known the real reason she would have politely suggested that I choose another subject.

I was never an artist as I am the Queen of stick-figures, but Miss Phelps always tried to bring out the best in me and everyone else. That year in grade 9 I won an award for art and still to this day have no idea why.

Almost fifty years later everyone remembers Miss Phelps and to some, like former CHS student Jim Manson, she became his mentor. In the Stanstead Journal in 2001

Manson gave an interview how she helped him with research when he was getting his PHD at Concordia.

He became engrossed in Samuel Willard who had spent many years petitioning the Quebec government for land owed to him in 1792. For two years Manson haunted the archives with Miss Phelps being the head historian cheerleader. Manson published a booklet and became part of the Brome County Historical Society and it was all thanks to our Miss Phelps. Jimmy Manson was not the only one that had fond memories of her and here are some comments from former students of Cowansville High School.

Claudia Forster Allen- Not only did I like Miss Phelps as a teacher for all obvious reasons as we've said before... her passion for history (local) and getting us to know our own history but she babysat me as a little girl when I was still crawling. It was in the apartment over the Dairy .. lol my parents lived there when they were first married. I would go in and immediately go for the cupboards and throw around and bang her pots and pans. She told me the story years later. I would also stand in the window and watch the cars go by. . . and pee my pants. . lol I think she lived with her mother and they would just laugh.

Audrey Bromby- I had her in 6th grade, and she was very quiet, soft spoken and very kind. She was in the Fordyce Women's Institute and used to come to our house when my mother had the meetings. I remember one time when she came, there was a painting on the wall done by my brother, Bob. She stood looking at it and said that she should have given him a better mark.

Bob Bromby- I recall that "piece of art", a still life bowl of fruit. I believe she gave me a 61% on it, which was close to the 59% FAIL and the worst mark in the class. Truth is that Miss Phelps drew most of it as she would frequently lean over my masterpiece and erase portions of my pitiful attempt to produce a classic and redraw it. She did this so many times that there was little of my 'blooming talent' left to see. The following year I went back to taking 'Gym' where I could at least clear the boxhorse. To this day I can draw a mean stick man. I only took the class at the urging of Stan Aiken (who did have talent) because he didn't want to be the only guy in the class. I wonder if that 'painting' is still around...

Wayne King- Loved her.

Barbara Goettel Lacroix- I had Miss Phelps in Grade 6. When she was writing on the blackboard, we used to copy each others' work!! I believe she was a bit hard of hearing also. She was a great art teacher - only year that I ever drew anything.

Margaret Clay Jacob- I also had Miss Phelps in Grade 6. I really don't remember that much about her actual teaching other than, as Audrey mentioned; she was soft spoken and kind. I loved her art classes and took them in Grade 9 & 10.

Linda Knight Seccaspina- She was one of the few teachers that believed in me.

Beverley Hastings Howman- I remember her art classes - my best subject. And the day Keith Bell posed for a full length pencil sketch (clothed of course). Good memories!

Claudia Forster Allen- it was, she was a lovely lady . . . inside and out . . . :)

Pennie Redmile- Not only was Miss Phelps a good teacher- but her love for local history caused her to "take on" the Quebec Goverment (about 20 years ago- - in her 80s) The Gov'ernor wanted to straighten the highway between Sweetsburg & West Shefford (Bromont) -- Near W Shefford, they were going to build their road over one of the earliest cemeteries. Miss Phelps was not about to allow that-- & she made her voice heard. Amazingly, the

Government heard her outrage-- & though they had no intention of changing their road's new location, they offered to put up a monument in the Methodist cemetery in West Shefford, with all the names & dates of the deceased from that old pioneer cemetery! Thanks to Miss Phelps intervention - that monument exists as a lasting memorial to some of the very early Shefford settlers!!

Pennie Redmile- With so many of her former students not living in the area, you may not know that every year there is a "Marion L Phelps Award" given to a person who has contributed a great deal to the preservation or promotion of local history in an area of Quebec. The first one went to Miss Phelps some years ago. I wasn't there to see her accept- but I was at the same conference & she was just "beaming". I'm not certain of the precise wording of the award-- but if no one else knows - I can find out.

There is also a series of books available on the Canada Archives & Library website called "Dictionary of Canadian Biography" & Miss Phelps contributed some of the articles about the earlier "folks".

Adelaide Lanktree- Miss Phelps is living at Manoir Lac Brome in Knowlton. I'm sure that she would love to hear how much she was appreciated. She is 103 years old.

Miss Phelps was actually born on a farm in South Stukely, Quebec, and graduated from Macdonald College with an intermediate teacher's diploma. Phelps has been given numerous awards throughout the years for her dedication to the history of the Eastern Townships but really it is the award of the heart that she deserves to get as she touched all of ours and will never be forgotten. Miss Phelps, there will never be a day where I or others forget what you brought to our lives and we thank you from the bottom of our hearts.

Thank you!

Chapter 22 - Final Words From the Facebook Group- "Those Darn Kids from Cowansville High School and Massey Vanier too"

The Final Question- What would you like everyone to remember about CHS?

Keith McClatchie- Those years were the best of my life! I am still best friends with a great number of classmates and I value those friendships over all else. I simply cannot believe that it has been over 50 years since I graduated from high school. I remember things as if it was just yesterday. My heart yearns to go back somehow but we know that that is impossible.

Carole Beattie- I started CHS in grade 5. Being an only child I loved going to school and every summer could hardly wait for September come around so I could see all my friends again. One of them that I met my first year here, Cyril, quickly became my close friend and later steady boyfriend and future husband. I really liked all of my teachers right through school - the "reading and writing and 'rithmetic". Those were some of the best years of my life and sometimes I wish I could just turn back the clock even for just a day. Yes, CHS holds a very special place in my heart and always will.

Audrey Bromby- I remember the long walks to catch the bus at the end of our road. My Grandkids always roll their eyes when I talk about it lol. I was painfully shy in my first years of elementary school. My cousin, Fay Rundel, introduced me to Karen Lee in grade one and we became fast friends since we were both shy. Noreen Dryden and Florence Elms became friends in grade school too...we were on the same school bus. We spent a lot of time at sleepovers back then. We still keep in touch. I also remember the school dances and watching American Bandstand after school whenever I could get the TV antenna to work. I couldn't wait every Fall when my mother took us shopping for new shoes and clothes. The first couple of months we didn't have to wear our tunics. I remember standing in line in the basement, waiting for the teacher to lead us upstairs. I can still hear the "clack clack clack" of Miss Spicer's high heeled shoes and couldn't wait until I could wear shoes like that one day. Good memories all in all.

Sheila Perry- I went to school in Cowansville for the 9th,10th, and 11th grade only, and coming from a very small town like Stanbridge East-to Cowansville at that time was overwhelming at times for me! Those 4 years(I had to repeat Grade 10) of my life were the best years of my teenage life along with my Nurses training in Montreal! My elementary years were troubled and CHS renewed my faith in the world and showed me that good things do happen! I made many friends that I still keep in contact with ,and all my experiences there were positive! I have nothing but fond memories when I see the letters CHS

Susan Jones Burnham- I remember all the athletics at CHS. We had intra-murals and all sorts of inter-scholastic sports teams. We always had high caliber athletes. The one-piece red gym outfit the girls had to wear left something to be desired, but even that did not deter us from achieving success. I have continued to be active throughout my life and it all started in a small town, in a school with a huge heart.

Beverly Mitchell- I went to CHS from grade one to grade seven and I didn't know then but I do know now they were the best years of my life I really enjoyed gym with Major Rubins as my phys. ed teacher he would allow us to try anything and those were my fond memories of him

Lynne Lang- I attended CHS for grades two through eleven. CHS was quite a change from grade one with two students in a two room schoolhouse in Dunham next door to my home. I remember Bill Busteed once commenting that we would look back on our school days as the best time in our lives. He was right. It holds special memories. At that time, school was our academic and social centre. In my children's time, community activities provided the social connection that CHS did for me. I can name all my teachers; something my children cannot do. My life has been great thanks in part to my years growing up in Dunham and attending Cowansville high School.

Valerie Lee-Fowler- I started grade one at CHS and went there up until the end of grade seven, then started grade eight at Massey Vanier. The friends that I made at CHS are still my friends today. I have fond memories of CHS and of the teachers. I remember Mrs. Thomas in grade one; she always wore her sweater buttoned up the back. I wondered why she wore it backwards. In grade four I remember sticking my hand in the ink well hole in my desk (yes I was a scrawny little thing). I had to have my teacher, Miss Wells, help me to get it out. Was I embarrassed!!! Grade seven with Mrs. Linkletter...what a year that was...I turned 13 on Friday the 13th and forgot my shoes at home that day (it was in December). I was scared to death of Mrs. Linkletter. Girls didn't have pierced ears like they do now, so us girls would take staples and fold them to make a triangle, add a couple more triangular staples, depending on how long we wanted our earrings, and then we'd put them on our earlobes...instant earrings. This worked really well until one of the girls had theirs a bit too long and Mrs. Linkletter saw them. Boy did we get a lecture about that!!! Oh the memories...I have so many good ones of CHS...I'll never forget my years there.

Claudia Forster Allen- Valerie, that was the style then, buttoned up the back! :)

Sheila Perry- I went to school in Cowansville for the 9th,10th., and 11th grade only, and coming from a very small town like Stanbridge East-coming to Cowansville at that time was overwhelming at times for me! Those 4 years(I had to repeat Grade 10) of my life were the best years of my teenage life along with my Nurses training in Montreal! My elementary years were troubled and CHS renewed my faith in the world and showed me that good things do happen! I made many friends that I still keep in contact with ,and all my experiences there were positive! I have nothing but fond memories when I see the letters CHS.

Margaret Clay Jacob I started CHS in 3rd grade as being from Farnham Centre, my 1st and 2nd grades were at the small one-room school house in East Farnham. About the only thing that I remember not liking about going to CHS was walking down the HWY to the corner when it was very cold. I would cry and my brother would tell me not to cry because my tears would freeze on face. I loved CHS, most of the teachers were good, made lots of friends and I especially enjoyed the school dances. I would run home from the bus stop, put the T.V. on American Bandstand with Dick Clark and learn all the newest dances. At the next school dance I would show off all my new moves and dance up a storm. I wasn't into sports but got my exercise by practicing the new dances and going to the school and church dances and show off what I'd learned. Another thing that I remember well was Remembrance Day ceremonies in front of the school with the laying on the wreaths and it always seemed to be cold or rainy and sometimes both but we didn't appreciate what it stood for until we were older. All in all, my years at CHS were some of the happiest and most fulfilling of my life...:)

Bob Bromby- The smell of Plasticine in grade one and the smell of the mimeograph chemical on the freshly printed exams and test papers, candy sales and 'Hot Dog Fridays' in the cafeteria and watching the clocks when the time changed in the spring and fall. Fire drills and Remembrance Day.......long time ago!

Brenda Snyder Stone-My memories of CHS –a school functioning at capacity between 1950-70. Amazing to me that my parents, Peggy Hastings and Gordon Snyder, had Miss Howard, (later married becoming Mrs. Shufelt,) the same grade one teacher as I. Then factor in that my brother Gregory and sister Heather, were also taught by her. Quite something. Guess we all must feel we have spent a lot of time standing in line—line up to go upstairs—line up to go downstairs—line up to get outside to line up for the buses—lining up to attend Memorial Services each November! The Johnny Jellybean show had a squawk-box, we had morning announcements, and hot lunch tickets. The Phys. Ed classes were rambunctious, the basketball teams truly admired, it seemed that the extracurricular activities were endless, and the bus trips to everywhere and anywhere we might escape to! I have memories of janitor Cerdric Henry giving roses to his favourite teacher of the day, from the stunning rose garden he cared for on the Davignon St lawn. The principal's office was small, so too the nurses quarters... There was no room—we ate in shifts in the cafeteria. Mrs. Reed, school nurse played an active role throughout the school year..I have memories of flu sweeping through the school, 6 or 7 of us sitting in class wondering how the 18 absentees were faring when a particularly ugly virus swept through town. The excitement of school dances, track and field days, Hylite committee meeting, the Red Cross Club, being volunteered for Student's council, the decorating committees, sewing grad dresses..and always a gaggle of yackers to pass judgement—smile.

Claudia Forster Allen- Excellent, Brenda . . .except Gr. 1 teacher started out as Miss Shufelt and became Mrs. Howard . . . lol they moved out west to live after they were married, as that is where he was from I believe. He boarded at her home for years and years . . . finally made her an "honest" woman . . lol No children came from that union . . . she was a darling woman and so patient and kind. Gordie and I had her and so did most of my mother's brothers and sisters. Except for "classes" I loved school. Loved the interchange and yacking. Loved the sports, loved the dances . . loved all the social part. Loved history and english classes, art, Home Ec, Miss Knowles another lovely person who was very talented. My husband noticed in the Hylite of my Graduation year that my "wish" was to get out of school and that my ambition was to be "Mr. Busteed's" secretary which I darn near was when I was a secretary at Massey-Vanier. For the most part, I have wonderful memories of my growing up a CHS.

Claudia Forster Allen- We were FAMILY! Something I miss down here in the east. It was evident at the Homecoming, all smiles and hugs and "lotsa yakking"!

Brenda Snyder Stone- Claudia - this is the second time I flipped her name around, please correct it for me before it gets any further! thanks..

Claudia Forster Allen-hahahahahha, too funny Brenda, but I understand, it's an age thing . .lol

Saturday at 12:08am · Unlike · 1

Bob Bromby- To be perfectly honest, I used to dread returning to classes at the end of summer. The summer end was marked by the Brome Fair which was always a major "hylite" (pun intended) but immediately after that event, the new school year commenced. It's not that school was that bad...but it wasn't that great either. Some teachers attempted to make learning fun but mostly not...No running in the halls...no chewing gum....sneakers in the gym but not in the classroom? After a summer of bike riding with friends all over the countryside, swimming in the pond or going to Bills Beach, working hard at hauling in the hay but playing just as hard, it was really hard to be enthusiastic about returning to school and 40 minute periods ended by that school bell. Many friends and acquaintances were made but few persisted over the years ...We all finally grew up.

Maureen Forster Page- My first day of school was in the old part in the front of the school, and quickly we were moved to the new addition. I remember loving the closets to hang our coats and a sink in the room. Also remember those horrible vitamin pills we were given to take. I used to run home at noon for lunch and run back just in time. Staying for lunch was a treat and also riding a bus. Later years was spent in Basketball practices, track and volleyball, loved it. Loved most of my elementary school teachers, although not so fond of some of my high school ones, except Mrs. Blinn.

David Hawke- I have fond memories but like Bob, but I dreaded the coming of Brome Fair and the return to the regime of senseless rules, guess that's why my academic record was less than stellar. I couldn't wait to get out of school, so I didn't live up to my potential. Actually, the classroom was time served in purgatory while waiting to be old enough to drive a truck. That said for the most part we had good teachers, good times & school spirit and I look back on those days with fondness.-----@Bob not really sure we all did grow up.

Bob Bromby Yes, I did finally grow up...I was about 42 years old when it occurred.

Linda Knight Seccaspina- Gee, I had to at least hit 46

Beverley Hastings Howman- I also started with Miss Shufelt. Kind lady. It was war time and we were busy collecting toothpaste tubes, and buying savings stamps. The early years were the best!

Claudia Forster Allen- Gee, guess I'm still growing . . . lol

Bob Bromby- Some of us just matured early.

David Hawke- I'm still trying to sell the last of my toys LOL

Linda Knight Seccaspina-Average in school, except for writing; I failed math every single year after my mother died in grade seven. One exam was so bad, I only got twenty nine out of two hundred in Grade 8 and my father queried if they also gave me marks for neatness.

I wanted to be like Jill Cady who got all A's on her report card and speak with million dollar words like Bobby

Perkins. Dragging a large personal caboose I would never excel in sports like Marianne Terauds and would forever be labeled as the one that almost failed gym.

One day I began to laugh and figured we were all really cool kids in school and just never figured it out. In the end maybe it was a good thing, because we learned to love ourselves and realized we did not need the acceptance of others to get by. I miss my past at CHS, but happy that those who were once in my life have now suddenly become my present and future.

Chapter 23 - Dedicated to Ed Moynan

Prayers to the family and hope he is found soon

Panama police suspect foul play in disappearance of retired Ottawa businessman

Article from the Ottawa Citizen

OTTAWA — A man who lived in Ottawa for more than 20 years has gone missing from his home in Panama — and Panamanian police suspect foul play.

Ed Moynan, 68, disappeared exactly a week ago from his home in Coronado, Panama. But, because his wife was visiting family in Ottawa, no one reported him missing until Saturday.

And, until Louise Moynan returned home on Monday, no one had noticed the subtle signs that a "violent struggle" took place before her husband disappeared.

Moynan, who owned Centennial Glass in Ottawa for more than two decades before retiring about two years ago, had taken his car into the shop on Thursday morning and was driving a rental car. The car is also missing but the door to his house was unlocked, the air conditioner which he usually only turns on when he's ready to go to sleep was left on, and his wallet and identification are both in the house.

Don Winner, who runs the English-language news website called Panama-guide.com, has lived in the Central American country for 25 years.

When a member of Panama's tight-knit expat community gets tied up in something bad — something where they have to go to police — they often go to Winner to help them "liaise with the authorities."

That's why Louise Moynan got in touch with Winner when she found out her husband had gone missing.

On Monday, Winner accompanied Louise Moynan and Ed Moynan's sister, Ruth, to the Direction of Judicial Information (Panama's national police force) to update the missing person's report.

Moynan told police that a centrepiece table in their foyer was out of place and scratched, their wooden-backed sofa had been scratched and broken, and Moynan's glasses — which he needs to wear at all times — were found broken on the floor.

"These are all the kinds of things that indicate a violent struggle has taken place," said Winner, who has been involved in many similar investigations in Panama.

The police were expected to send a forensics team to the house Thursday to fingerprint the area, search for trace evidence and do luminol testing in which police spray a substance to find traces of human blood that has been cleaned up and is therefore invisible to the human eye.

Winner said police seem to be doing all they can to push the investigation forward.

Although police and the family is withholding some details central to the case, they have released some pieces that point to foul play.

The same day Moynan disappeared, he did a neighbour a favour that might seem strange in Canada but is apparently "very common" in Panama.

A Swiss neighbour who wanted to visit his son in Europe asked Moynan to use his credit card to buy a $1,500 plane ticket online. Once the transaction went through, the neighbour gave Moynan $1,500 in cash.

"It may seem strange," said Winner, "but there are a lot of people in Panama under what you might consider weird circumstances" and many of them either don't want to have a credit card or can't.

Winner said it's not the transaction that worries him, but the fact that Moynan would have had that much cash in his pocket.

"Every time I have more than a couple of hundred dollars on me, I get nervous. I want to put it in the bank."

He said he doesn't know what happened in this situation but, in similar circumstances a victim might have been seen pulling large amounts of cash from a bank machine and then been followed.

"If someone saw the money changing hands, they would have known Ed had it."

Winner said he thinks the case will "break open" once the authorities find Moynan's rental car — a 2012 grey Kia Rio, licence number 975349.

"His disappearance is tied to that car, and, let's face it, it's a lot easier to find a car than a man."

Canada's Department of Foreign Affairs and National Trade would not confirm anything except that is was "providing consular assistance to the family of the Canadian citizen who has been reported missing in Panama" and was in "ongoing contact with local authorities."

tesmith@ottawacitizen.com

twitter.com/tsmithjourno

With files from Zev Singer and Shaamini Yogaretnam

Chapter 24 - The 2012 Class Reunion

On Labour Day weekend of 2012 worlds collided and the former students of Cowansville High School met once again. There were no dunk tanks, nor ill words spoken about times gone by. If you look at the Facebook page "Those Darn Kids From Cowansville High School" there was nothing but smiles in those photos and let's hope we all attend another one.

Sadly, I could not make it as I was sitting on an Amtrack train for 4 days, but hope to see some of you another year. Thanks to all that put this together, as without you it would not have happened. I am going to add this short story I found on the web in 2006 waiting for the day I could post it.

By Anonymous

I had prepared for it like any intelligent woman would. I went on a starvation diet the day before, knowing that all the extra weight would just melt off in 24 hours, leaving me with my sleek, trim, high-school-girl body.

The last many years of careful cellulite collection would just be gone with a snap of a finger. I knew if I didn't eat a morsel on Friday, then could probably fit into my senior formal on Saturday.

Trotting up to the attic, I pulled the gown out of the garment bag, carried it lovingly downstairs, ran my hand over the fabric, and hung it on the door. I stripped naked, looked in the mirror, sighed, and thought, "Well, okay, maybe if I shift it all to the back. . . . bodies never have pockets where you need them."

Bravely, I took the gown off the hanger, unzipped the shimmering dress and stepped gingerly into it. I struggled, twisted, turned, and pulled and I got the formal all the way up to my knees before the zipper gave out. I was disappointed. I wanted to wear that dress with those silver platform sandals again and dance the night away. Okay, one setback was not going to spoil my mood for this affair. No way! Rolling the dress into a ball and tossing it into the corner, I turned to Plan B: the black velvet caftan.

I gathered up all the goodies that I had purchased at the drug store: the scented shower gel, the body building and highlighting shampoo & conditioner, and the split-end killer and shine enhancer.

Soon my hair would look like that girl's in the Pantene ads. Then the makeup -- the under eye "ain't no lines here" firming cream, the all-day face-lifting gravity-fighting moisturizer with wrinkle filler spackle; the all day "kiss me till my lips bleed, and see if this gloss will come off" lipstick, the bronzing face powder for that special glow . . .

But first, the roll-on facial hair remover. I could feel the wrinkles shuddering in fear. OK - time to get ready. I jumped into the steaming shower, soaped, lathered, rinsed, shaved, tweezed, buffed, scrubbed, and scoured my body to a tingling pink. I plastered my freshly scrubbed face with the anti-wrinkle, gravity fighting, "your face will look like a baby's butt" face cream. I set my hair on the hot rollers. I felt wonderful.

Ready to take on the world. Or in this instance, my underwear.

With the towel firmly wrapped around my glistening body, I pulled out the black lace, tummy-tucking, cellulite-pushing, ham hock-rounding girdle, and the matching "lifting those bosoms like they're filled with helium" bra.

I greased my body with the scented body lotion and began the plunge. I pulled, stretched, tugged, hiked, folded, tucked, twisted, shimmied, hopped, pushed, wiggled, snapped, shook, caterpillar crawled, and kicked.

Sweat poured off my forehead but I was done. And it didn't look bad. So I rested. A well deserved rest too. The girdle was on my body. Bounce a quarter off my behind? It was tighter than a trampoline. Can you say, "Rubber baby buggy bumper butt? Okay, so I had to take baby steps, and walk sideways, and I couldn't move from my butt cheeks to my knees. But I was firm!

Oh no . . . I had to go to the bathroom! And there wasn't a snap crotch. From now on, undies gotta have a snap crotch. I was ready to rip it open and re-stitch the crotch with Velcro, but the pain factor from past experiments was still fresh in my mind. I quickly sidestepped to the bathroom. An hour later, I had answered nature's call and repeated the struggle into the girdle.

Then I was ready for the bra. I remembered what the saleslady said to do. I could see her glossed lips mouthing, "Do not fasten the bra in the front and twist it around. Put the bra on the way it should be worn -- straps over the shoulders. Then bend over and gently place both breasts inside the cups."

Easy if you have four hands.

But, with confidence, I put my arms into the holsters, bent over and pulled the bra down, but the boobs weren't cooperating. I'd no sooner tuck one in a cup, and while placing the other, the first would slip out. I needed a strategy.

I bounced up and down a few times, tried to dribble them in with short bunny hops, but that didn't work. So, while bent over, I began rocking gently back and forth on my heel and toes and I set 'em to swinging. Finally on the fourth swing, pause, and lift, I captured the gliding glands. Quickly fastening the back of the bra, I stood up for examination. Back straight, slightly arched, I turned and faced the mirror, turning front, and then sideways. I smiled.

Yes, Houston, we have lift up!

My breasts were high, firm, and there was cleavage! Cleavage! I was happy until I tried to look down. I had a chin rest. And I couldn't see my feet. I still had to put on my pantyhose, and shoes. Oh, why did I buy heels with buckles?

Then I had to pee again.

Everything came off, and I put on my sweats, fixed myself a drink, ordered pizza, and . . . . . skipped the reunion.

Chapter 24 - HS Homecoming Thank You Letter - by Claudia Forster-Allen

Sunday, Sept. 2nd, 2012

It all started when Audrey Bromby and Linda Knight-Seccaspina put a Group page on FB entitled "Those Darn Kids from CHS and maybe Massey-Vanier". The rest is history. Through the chit chat and many stories from the past someone suggested a Reunion was in order. How many were interested? A few hits but enough to say okay let's do it by John Staton, Dave Hawke and Claudia Forster-Allen. Away we went and the ideas started to roll. Where should we have it there isn't much time, how about a booth at Brome Fair and we can all meet. Well, we all know what happened in the end. . it became much bigger and the momentum built with each day.

There are many people to thank for their help and efforts and dedication to the event. Not to mention the comments and pictures from the past on Facebook, which kept things interesting. It came about that any monies we would make would go the "Heroes Memorial Elementary School Breakfast Program": Cowansville Legion Branch 99:

Robert Bouthot – President, without his approval and positive outlook and the generosity to let us have the event there and for FREE was amazing. What a great venue it proved to be. My ideas were accepted and there wasn't anything they would not do for us to make it happen. I was told that Heroes was their school and we could have anything we wished. That opened the door to more ideas.

Also like to thank, Robert's wife Vicky and his Sergeant at Arms. They got together and made the lasagna supper and worked very hard to make it happen. Delicious too . .

Thanks to the "Colour Party" who donated their time to help make the Remembrance Day ceremony a success.

To Deputy Mayor of C'ville – Ghislain Valliere

To Rev. Han, who came and led us in prayer.

To Ron Vail, who called out the Honour Roll

Our Wreath Layers -

Ghislain Valliere - Town of Cowansville

Jean Scott – Silver Cross Mother

Ron Vail – Veterans of all Wars

Richard Staples – Teacher '67-'69 honouring our classmates and friends from CHS - deceased

Keith McClatchie – Master of Ceremonies for all events and entertainment

Next Big Thank you goes to Heroes Memorial Elem. School:

Louise Smith for her part in co-ordinating everything which took place at the school for our welcome tour and memorabilia.

The people who took part are as follows:

Terry Bell – Principal for allowing us entry to the school.

Perry Mason – set up gym

Rodney Smith – opened the building and all the doors

Teachers:

Rosemary Scott – cover for the autograph book

Susan Burnham – Legion info and helped set up books

Danny Lapointe – photographer

Lisa Bates – polished trophies

All Homeroom Teachers – cards for the homecoming

TourGuides:

Students – Angel Hebert, Jaysin Sornberger-Tetrault, Jayden Perry, Malena Perkins, Olivia Dumont - they did a great job and heard some wild stories . . . .

Singers: - Ember Gendreau, Nathaniel Beattie, Vivianne Beaulac. What a wonderful job they did at the ceremony "They are Heroes".

Music – Laura Barr and Louise Smith

They made the reunion such a success and I thank them all from the bottom of my heart. What a great job and did themselves proud.

Legion Festivities

Luncheon Co-ordinators & Set Up – Margaret Clay-Jacob & Barb Goettel

Thank you ladies for organizing and setting it up. Thank you to all who donated food and there are many. It was much appreciated and delicious.

CHS Homecoming Cake – Judy Bruhmuller-Nadeau – awesome & delicious!

Raffle & Silent Auction –thank you to all who donated – to name a few Sheila Perry, Wendy Labrecque's neighbour, Kelly Reagan, Wendy Labrecque, David /Dave,Sandy Castle-TenEyck, Jean Beattie, Judy Bruhmuller, Deserie Phillips, Noreen Dryden, Gerry Bougie (husband to Edwina Jennie), Noreen Dryden. I hope I didn't miss anyone. Geoff Allen for taking care of the raffle. Charlie Christie for "calling out" the Silent Auction Winners.

To everyone who bought tickets on the two raffles and the winners of the Silent Auction . . A huge thank you as we raised over $700 towards the Breakfast Programme.

The Legion for donating their profits from the supper, $302.

Linda Knight-Seccaspina who is donating the proceeds on the book she is writing and due out in the near future entitled " Cowansville High School Misremembered" in memory of her sister Robin Knight Nutbrown.

Entertainment: Keith McClatchie, Marriette McClatchie, Walter Shufelt.

Judy Pickle – for her input and putting me in contact with the school and other much needed info and her positive attude and cheering me onwards . . .

Jean Beattie – for her help in contacting the Reverand Han and generally feeding me much needed information from Cowansville. She was a great "go-to" person and willing to go the mile including the card to Miss Phelps.

All my volunteer Booth Sitters and setter-uppers and taker-downers.

John Staton, Jean Beattie, Dale Brock, Keith McClatchie, Dave Hawke, Larry McCrum, ValerieLee-Fowler, Sheila & Walt Shufelt, John F arrell, John Griffiths and all others who dropped in and helped out and chatted.

To all of you who showed up and showed your support and had a good time. Thanks to Facebook who made it all possible .. social media works.

Thank you one and all for your participation as you made it the success that it turned out to be. It was great to all be together and have fun and get in touch with each other once again.

I truly appreciate all that everyone did to help make it a success.
Sincerely,

Claudia Forster-Allen

Guest Book - Homecoming CHS 2012

1. Claudia Forster-Allen - PEI

2. Margaret Clay-Jacob - Quebec

3. Dale Brock - Quebec

4. Dawn Brock - Quebec

5. Dave Corey -

6. Judy Bruhmuller-Nadeau - Quebec

7. Norma Sherrer- Quebec

8. Beverley Howman - USA

9. Peggy Hastings-Snyder-Bailey - Quebec

10. Rodney Jenne - Quebec

11. Alan Webb - Quebec

12. Crystal Royea-McAleer - Quebec

13. Keith McClatchie & Marriette - Ontario

14. Micheline Farkas - Canada

15. Shirley Miltimore - Quebec

16. John Staton - Quebec

17. Steve Trew - Quebec

18. Larry McCrum & Wendy - USA

19. Peter Enright - Quebec

20. Chuck/Charlie Christie - Quebec

21. Roger Durrell - Quebec

22. Gary Scott - Ontario

23. Joanne Lafleur - Quebec

24. Gail Persons - Quebec

25. Claire (Christie) Ontario

26. Geraldine (Mahannah) Jourdenais- Quebec

27. Carmen Taylor- Quebec

28. Johnny Taylor - Quebec

29. David Peacock - USA

30. Don Phillips - Ontario

31. Peter Boast - Quebec

32. Stanley Shover - Quebec

33. Douglas Farr - Ontario

34. Glen McCrum - BC

35. Sandra (Forster) Alston - NB

36. Renee Campeau Wilson -Quebec

37. Marjorie & Roland Horner -Ontario

38. Robert Forster - Ontario

39. Cynthia (Allen) Fudakowski -Ontario

40. Tom Fudakowski- Ontario

41. Valerie Fowler (Lee) - USA

42, Eva Dobbin-Terauds

43. Marc Tevyaw - Ontario

44. Sheila Perry-Shufelt - New Brunswick

45. David Bromby - Quebec

46. David Haines - Quebec

47. Jean Scott - Quebec

48. Wayne Scott - Ontario

49. Brenda Scott-Royer & Donald - Quebec

50. Karen Moreton-Wright -Quebec

51. Walter Shufelt - Quebec

52. Wesley Mason (Wendy) - Quebec

53. Blair Bowles - Quebec

54. John Griffiths - Ontario

55. Susan Bowles-Hunter - British Columbia

56. Janice Buzzell Allen- Quebec

57. Barbara Goettel Lacroix - Quebec

58. Manuel Greig,- Quebec

59. Brenda Snyder Stone - Quebec

60. Bob Scott (Pam Stuart) - Ontario

61. Beverly Mitchell - Quebec

62. Noel Mitchell (Beyea)-Quebec

63. John Hodge - Quebec

64. Dave Harvey - Quebec

65. Martha Lickfold - Quebec

66. Tim Lickfold - Ontario

67. Cindy Rhicard - Quebec

68. Joan Mewett-Lunn - Ontario

69. Roberta Barnes-Boudreau -Quebec

70. Ken Bell - Quebec

71. Betty ?Tevyaw- Quebec

72. Don Lunn- Ontario

73. Roy Bromby-Quebec

74. Christal Golasowski- Quebec

75. Victor & Paulette Mahannah-Quebec

76. Roger & Anne Page- Quebec

77. John Farrell-Ontario

78. Bruce Lickfold - Quebec

79. Steven Page - Quebec

80. Michael C. Lewis - Quebec

81. John Bruhmuller - Quebec

82. Valerie Ethier-Cameron - Quebec

83. Harris Shufelt - Quebec

84. Linda Mewett

85. Judy Bromby - Quebec

86. Cindy Christie- Quebec

87. Jean Beattie - Quebec

88. Allan Wilson - Quebec

89. Bill Stocks - USA

90. Valerie & John Hunter -Quebec

91. Judith Pickel - Quebec

92. Janet King - Quebec

93. Wayne King

94. Gary Farr - Quebec

95. Peter Boast -Quebec

96. David Haines - Quebec

97. George Cote (King) - Quebec

98. L (?) - Brome, Quebec

99. Brenda Mahannah Ladd - Quebec

100. Pat Lickfold - Quebec

101. Noreen Dryden - Quebec

102. Bill Busteed - Quebec

103. Ken Bell - Quebec

104. Marvin Beattie - Quebec

105. Susan Burnham- Jones - Quebec

106. Gavin Beattie (?) - Quebec

107. Edna King-Chagnon - USA

108. Beverly Mitchell - Quebec

109. Gary Labrecque - Quebec

110. Marvin Scott - Quebec

111. Betty Castle - Quebec

112. Douglas Farr - Ontario

113. Walter & Sheila (Perry)- Shufelt -New Brunswick

114. David Hawke- Playa San Diego, La Libertad, El Salvador

Former CHS Students Who Are No Longer With Us - May They Rest in Peace

1. Paul Jordan
2. Paul Hamm
3. Joyce Palmer
4. Pam Doherty
5. Cindy Harvey
6. Gerry Blinn
7. Ted Nagano
8. Susan Turner
9. Bill Joa
10. Norm Burnham
11. Terry Page
12. Blair Bowling [Mar.12,2011]
13. Malcolm Bowling (1940-1958)
14. Russell Rhycard
15. Fred Aston
16. Arnold TenEyck
17. Robin Knight Nutbrown
18. Kenny Bowles
19. Tom Dryden (2009)
20. Barbara Dougall [Dec.10, 2008]
21. Stephen Perkins
22. Bobby Kelly
23. Michael Clark
24. Debbie Lickfold,
25. Murray Perkins
26. Steven Stott

27. Arthur Poll
28. Judy-Bell Johnson
29. Floyd Johnson
30. Wayne Bates
31. Dale Stott
32. Leslie Sherrer
33. Gower Bradshaw
34. Steven Paul
35. Heather Luce
36. Julie Bradshaw
37. Dennis McCullough
38. Kevin Harvey
39. Stanley Aitken
40. Nona Hadlock
41. Jack Perrott
42. Andy Goettel
43. Gordon Corey
44. Audrey Corey
45. Susan Desruisseaux
46. Peter Dempster
47. Rolland Sherrer
48. Grant Luce
49. Dennis Brown
50. Greg Snyder
51. Randall Sargent
52. Gordon McGuigan
53. Lacey Forster (4 Nov 2002)
54. Peter Shufelt
55. Wayne Rumbolt
56. Robert Kerr
57. Judy Pride
58. Bev Ingalls

59. Ronnie Allen

60. Jimmy Palmer

61. Frank Elms

62. Larry Clark

63. Kathleen Elms

64. Norman Wilson

65. Walter Alchovy

66. Gordon Butler

67. Opal Kinsella

68. Douglas Dryden (Sept.20, 2011)

69. Rory Mitchell

70. Jean Marilyn Algier

71. Keith Scott

72. Richard Parent

73. Edith Horner Shufelt

74. Isabel Cramer

75. Graham Sharman

76. John Fregeau

77. Barry Fregeau

78. Larry Wetherby

79. Frances Beattie

80. Gary Bromby[Jan.28,1998]

81. Richard (Dickie) Taylor

82. Douglas (Bud) Taylor (1927-2002)

83. Cyril Beattie

84. Pat Moxon (Feb. 13, 2012)

85. Dale Larose (April 28, 2006)

86. Nora Howard

87. Audrey Lewis

88. Jeannine Downs

89. Richard [Dickie] Barratt [Nov.13, 2011]

90. Tommy Wenkert

91. Trevor David

92. Kenny Farr

93. Mary (Christine) Lickfold (Apr.28, 2007)

94. Pauline (Polly) Jenne (Nov.27, 2010)

95. Bunny Selby

96. Rolland Hall

97. Joan Sharman

98. Aija Terauds (Nov. 1, 2011)

99. Ruth (Mahannah) Hawke, student & teacher (Jan. 19, 2011)

100. Geraldine Lickfold

101. Joyce Lickfold-Jodoin

102. Beverley Ann Ingalls (nee: Sanford) Nov.5, 2011.

103. Peggy Hawke-Vail

104. Winston (Charlie) Rundel

105. Norman Rundel

107. Keith Rundel

108. Galt Brown

109. Gordon Snyder

110. Otis Hall

111. Albert Jameson

112. Rory Mitchell

113. Desmond King

114. Johnny Brown

115. Carol Bracey

116. Claude Arpin

117 Angela Gage

118 David Lang

119 Violet (Dennis) King

120 Morris Grenier

121 Gerald Grenier

122. Ardice Buchanan

123. Barbara Beattie

124. Paul Archer

125. Bob Douglas

126. Douglas Smith

127. Keith Mitchell

128. Kathleen Mitchell

129. Sandra Brown (May 16th, 2012)

130. George Phillips

131. Gary Phillips

132. Lawrence Phillips

133. Gloria Rowse Bowles

134. Buddy Bowles

135. Douglas Rowse

136. Murray Rowse

137. Timmy Longtin

138. Algie Narbutus

139. Johnny Grenier

140. Harry Bell (Harry's Pool Room of fame) 1971

141. Nancy Howard (MacMillan)

142. Edward "Buzz" McCrum

143. Greg Sylvester and family (car accident-

Greg& son Connor Aug.18, 1999, wife Anne Aug. 19, 1999)

144. Edith Hastings

145. Ruth Hastings

146. Howard Hastings

147. Hope Cotton-Jenne

148. Doug Stocks

149. Jack Stocks

150. Claude King

151. Noella Graham

152. Christopher Zucrowski

153, Harold Pickle

154. Helen Pickle

155. Eric Smith

156. Gary Brock 1960

157. Maureen Fee

158. James Fee

159. Vollen Hastings

160. Fred Tanner

161. Collin Booth

162. Barbara Goheen

163. Audrey Strange

164. Beryl Henry

165. Alice Longway

166. Doreen Longway

167. John T. Webster

168. Lois Webster -Ford

169. Richard (Ricky) Johnson (Aug 10, 2012)

170. Garth Dean

171. Tony Royea

172. Julie Bradshaw

173. Greg Snyder

174. Gordon Darby (CHS & Massey-Vanier)

175. Norma Ford

176. Ken Ford

177. Michael Longeway

178. Alexander Zukrowski

179. Mary McCutcheon

180. Tommy Graham

181. Byron Hall

182. Roger Ten Eyke - Sept 19 2012

183. David/Dwight Jacob

184. Fredrick Charles "Charlie" Taylor -Sept. 28, 1938 - Oct. 21, 2012 RIP

185. Huzon Grenier

186. Bruce Watt

Deceased Fallen Veterans from Cowansville High School

1. Dempsey Forster
2. Alfie Forster
3. Bert Forster
4. Larry Labrecque
5. Reginald Hawke
6. Bill McClatchie
7. Barney Johnston
8. Gerry Johnston
9. Bud Bromby
10. Jack Bromby
11. Pete Fillion
12. Ronald Perry
13. Clifford Morin(both World Wars)
14. Darcy Morin
17. Maurice Webb
21. Leonard Lickfold
22. Albert Moore
23. Charlie Wyatt
24. Eric Fulford
25. Harry Redmile
26. Bill Craigie
27. ? Heatherington
28. Norman Brock
29. Keith Scott
30. Ken Scott
31. Francis Scott

32. Doug Hawke? (captive in a Japanese concentration camp, survived and died at home)

33. Raymond Farrell

34. George Fernihough

35. Charlie Cromack (WWI)

36. Lawrence "Bud" Lee

37. Fred Pettes (WWII)

38. Orville Bromby

39. John Bowling

40. David Watt

41. John Miller

42. Frederick Garth Hall (Seaman WW2)

43. Murray Wallet

44. G. William Webster

45. Garth Dean

46. Arthur Knight